First World War
and Army of Occupation
War Diary
France, Belgium and Germany

42 DIVISION
125 Infantry Brigade,
Brigade Machine Gun Company
1 March 1917 - 28 February 1918

WO95/2655/3

The Naval & Military Press Ltd
www.nmarchive.com
Published in association with The National Archives

Published by

The Naval & Military Press Ltd

Unit 10 Ridgewood Industrial Park,

Uckfield, East Sussex,

TN22 5QE England

Tel: +44 (0) 1825 749494

www.naval-military-press.com

www.nmarchive.com

This diary has been reprinted in facsimile from the original. Any imperfections are inevitably reproduced and the quality may fall short of modern type and cartographic standards.

© Crown Copyright
Images reproduced by permission of The National Archives, London, England, 2015.

Contents

Document type	Place/Title	Date From	Date To
Heading	WO95/2655/3 125 Bde MG Coy.-42 Div Mar 1917-Feb 1918		
Heading	42nd Division 125th Infy Bde 125th Machine Gun Coy. Mar 1917-Feb 1918		
Heading	War Diary of the 125th Machine Gun Coy. From March 1st, 1917 to March 31st 1917 (Volume III) Vol 2		
War Diary	France Macon	01/03/1917	02/03/1917
War Diary	Pont Remy	02/03/1917	02/03/1917
War Diary	Ref Trap Fourth army area administrative Trap Sheet 2 Scale 1: 100000	03/03/1917	03/03/1917
War Diary	Fontainesur Somme	04/03/1917	07/03/1917
War Diary	France Fontaine Ref. Map Fourth Army Area Administrative Map Sheet 2 Scale 1:100,000	07/03/1917	09/03/1917
War Diary	Fontaine-Sur Somme	10/03/1917	12/03/1917
War Diary	Ref. Trap Fourth army area administrative Trap Sheet 2 Scale 1: 100000	13/03/1917	15/03/1917
War Diary	Corbie Ref. Trap Sheet 62 1., Scale 1/100000	15/03/1917	15/03/1917
War Diary	France Hamel Ref. Trap Sheet 62 D Col 1. Scale 1/40000 P.10.a	15/03/1917	25/03/1917
War Diary	Frise Sheet 62c Col 1. Scale 1/40000 G.18.d.	26/03/1917	31/03/1917
Diagram etc	Fontaine-S-Somme Appendix I		
Miscellaneous	Extracts from Operation Order 26 Appendix II	13/03/1917	13/03/1917
Operation(al) Order(s)	125th Machine Gun Company Order No. 27	14/03/1917	14/03/1917
Diagram etc	Hamel Appendix IV		
Diagram etc	Frise Appendix V		
Heading	War Diary of the 125th Machine Gun Coy. from April 1st 1917 to April 30th 1917. (Volume IV)		
War Diary	France Frise Ref. Trap Sheet 62c Col I. Scale 1/40000 G. 18.d.	01/04/1917	07/04/1917
War Diary	Ref. Trap 62c Scale 1/40000 I.27.b.8.6	08/03/1917	09/03/1917
War Diary	E. 25.b.2.8	09/04/1917	10/04/1917
War Diary	Ref. Trap 62c N.E. Scale 1/20000 F.1.a.b.	11/04/1917	12/04/1917
War Diary	France. Ref. Maps. 57c. S.E. 62c. N.E. Scale 1/20000	12/04/1917	15/04/1917
War Diary	France. Ref. Maps. 57c. S.E. 62c. N.E. Scale 1/20000 Ref. Trap 62c 1/40000	16/04/1917	20/04/1917
War Diary	France Ref. Maps 62c 1/40000	20/04/1917	20/04/1917
War Diary	Frise	21/04/1917	22/04/1917
War Diary	Peronne	23/04/1917	24/04/1917
War Diary	France Ref. Map 62c 1/40000 Peronne I. 27.b.	25/04/1917	29/04/1917
War Diary	Ref. Traps 62c N.E. 1/20000 Tincourt	30/04/1917	30/04/1917
Miscellaneous	Appendix I	02/05/1917	02/05/1917
Miscellaneous	Appendix II	02/05/1917	02/05/1917
Miscellaneous	Staff Captain, 126 Brigade	04/04/1917	04/04/1917
Miscellaneous	From transport officers, 125th Coy M.G. Corps. to adjt. 125th Coy. M.G. Corps.	04/04/1917	04/04/1917
Miscellaneous	From transport officers, 125 Coy M.G. Corps. to adjt. 125 Coy. M.G. Corps.	13/04/1917	13/04/1917
Miscellaneous Map	Tactical and Technical Lessons learnt during frast month	21/04/1917	21/04/1917
Miscellaneous	Brigade Front		

Heading	War Diary. of The 125th Machine Gun Coy. From May 1st, 1917 to May 31st, 1917. (Volume. V.) Vol 4		
War Diary	France Tincourt. Ref. Maps. 20.000 Sheet 62c NE. Ed. 3A. K. 19.a.1.8	01/05/1917	07/05/1917
War Diary	Longavesnes E. 25.6.3.3	08/05/1917	08/05/1917
War Diary	France. Longauesnes E.25.b.3.3	09/05/1917	09/05/1917
War Diary	Peziere. W. 30d. 8.8	10/05/1917	18/05/1917
War Diary	France Dynamite Wood. Villers Faucon.	19/05/1917	20/05/1917
War Diary	V. II.a.	21/05/1917	22/05/1917
War Diary	W. I.b. 5.5	23/05/1917	27/05/1917
War Diary	Ytres. P.20.6.5.2	28/05/1917	29/05/1917
War Diary	France P.20.b.5.2	29/05/1917	31/05/1917
Operation(al) Order(s)	125th Brigade. Order No. 11 Appendix A.	30/04/1917	30/04/1917
Miscellaneous	Table to Accompany 125th Brigade Order Number 11		
Operation(al) Order(s)	125th. Brigade Order No. 12. Appendix "B"	03/05/1917	03/05/1917
Operation(al) Order(s)	125th Brigade O.O. No. 14 Appendix "C"	06/05/1917	06/05/1917
Miscellaneous	Table to Accompany 125th Brigade O.O. No 14		
Operation(al) Order(s)	125th. Brigade O.O. No. 16. Appendix "D"	16/05/1917	16/05/1917
Miscellaneous	Table to Accompany 125th Brigade O.O. No. 16		
Miscellaneous	Administrative Instructions No. 3. Issued in Connection With Brigade O.O. No. 16	15/05/1917	15/05/1917
Operation(al) Order(s)	125th Brigade O.O. No 17 Appendix "E"		
Operation(al) Order(s)	Addendum No to 125th Brigade O.O. No. 16		
Miscellaneous	March Table To Accompany 125th Brigade OO No 17		
Operation(al) Order(s)	125 Brigade Warning Order No 18 Appendix "F"	20/05/1917	20/05/1917
Operation(al) Order(s)	125. Brigade O.O. No. 19 Appendix "G"	24/05/1917	24/05/1917
Operation(al) Order(s)	Addendum Number 1. To 125 Brigade O.O. Number 19 Appendix "H"	27/05/1917	27/05/1917
Heading	War Diary of The 125th Machine Gun Coy. From June 1st, 1917 to June 30th, 1917. (Volume VI) Vol 5		
War Diary	France Ytres P20 b 5.2. Sheet 57c SE & NE 1/20,000	01/06/1917	06/06/1917
War Diary	Q 13 d.8.8	07/06/1917	09/06/1917
War Diary	France Q 13 d.8.8. Sheet 57c SE 1 SW 2 NE 3 NW 4 1/10000	09/06/1917	11/06/1917
War Diary	France Q13d 8.8	12/06/1917	22/06/1917
War Diary	Ytres P. 20.C.3.1. 1/40000	22/06/1917	27/06/1917
War Diary	France Ytres P.20.C.3.7 1/40000	30/06/1917	30/06/1917
Miscellaneous	Preliminary Instructions Appendix "B"	24/06/1917	24/06/1917
Map	Appendix C		
Miscellaneous	Tactical And Technical Lessons Learnt During June 1917. Appendix D.		
Heading	War Diary of 125 Machine Gun. Coy. For July 1917. Vol VII		
War Diary	France Map. Ref. Sheet 57c P.20 G. 3.7. 1/40,000	01/07/1917	06/07/1917
War Diary	A. 29.a.5.1	07/07/1917	09/08/1917
War Diary	A. 29 b 7.5	10/07/1917	10/07/1917
Heading	War Diary for 125th Machine Gun Company. From August 1st. 1917 to August 31st. 1917. (Volume VIII)		
War Diary	France Map. Ref. Sheet 57c. 1/40,000 A. 29.b.7.5	01/08/1917	20/08/1917
War Diary	Lens 11. 1/1000.000 H.6	21/08/1917	22/08/1917
War Diary	Sheet 27 W.2. 1/40,000 L.13.d.3.4	23/08/1917	25/08/1917
War Diary	France	26/08/1917	28/08/1917
War Diary	Sheet 28 1/40,000 L.16.a.9.5	29/08/1917	30/08/1917
War Diary	Sheet 28. N.E.1. Sheet 28. N.W.2. 1/10,000	30/08/1917	31/08/1917
Miscellaneous	125th Machine Gun Company. Appendix "B"	21/08/1917	21/08/1917

Miscellaneous	Statement Shewing Strength Of Company, Casualties Etc. Appendix "C".		
Heading	War Diary for 125th Machine Gun Company, From September 1st 1917 to September 30th. 1917 Volume IX		
War Diary	France Map Reference. Sheet Frezenberg 1/10000	01/09/1917	02/09/1917
War Diary	28. N.E. 1	02/09/1917	02/09/1917
War Diary	28 N.W. 1 1/20000	03/09/1917	05/09/1917
War Diary	France	06/09/1917	30/09/1917
Miscellaneous	Report "A".		
Miscellaneous	Tactical And Technical Lessons Learnt.	21/09/1917	21/09/1917
Map	Trenches Corrected From Information Received Up To 21.8.17		
Map	Appendix "A"		
Operation(al) Order(s)	Move Order No. 7 By Captain R.V. Gery. Commanding "Jangle"	28/02/1917	28/02/1917
Operation(al) Order(s)	125th Brigade Operation Order Number 35	04/09/1917	04/09/1917
Miscellaneous	Time Table For 24 Guns Firing On Langemarck Gheluvelt Line		
Miscellaneous	Statement Shewing Strength OF Company, Casualties ETC. Appendix		
Miscellaneous	Results of Operations	30/09/1917	30/09/1917
Miscellaneous	125th Inf. Bde.	03/09/1917	03/09/1917
Miscellaneous	Time Table For 24 Guns Firing On To Langemark-Gheluvelt Line.		
Miscellaneous	125th Brigade Instructions Number 2	04/09/1917	04/09/1917
Heading	War Diary For 125th Machine Gun Company, From October 1st, 1917 To October 31st., 1917		
War Diary	Map. Ref. Furnes 1/40000 W.5.d. Central	01/10/1917	06/10/1917
War Diary	Map. No. 5 Niea Port 1/10000	07/10/1917	09/10/1917
War Diary	No. Snieuport. 1/10000	10/10/1917	22/10/1917
War Diary	Furnes 1/40000 W.18.d.55	23/10/1917	30/10/1917
War Diary	Map. Ref. Furnes 1/4000. 55 W/sd.	30/10/1917	31/10/1917
Miscellaneous	Relief Orders By Captain, K.V. C E R, Y, Commanding "Rain" Appendix A	06/10/1917	06/10/1917
Miscellaneous	125th Machine Gun Coy. S.O.S. Liens. Appendix B	20/10/1917	20/10/1917
Map	Appendix B.		
Operation(al) Order(s)	Order No. 1. Relief Orders by Captain G.C. Kay. Commanding 125 A.G. Coy. Appendix C.	17/10/1917	17/10/1917
Operation(al) Order(s)	Order No. 2. by Capt. G.C. Kay Commanding 125 M.G. Coy. Appendix D		
Operation(al) Order(s)	Order No. 3. by Capt. G.C. Kay Commanding 125 M.G. Coy. Appendix E.		
Operation(al) Order(s)	Order No. 4 by Capt. G.C. Kay Commanding 125 M.G. Coy. Appendix E.	21/10/1917	21/10/1917
Miscellaneous	To 125th Infantry Brigade. Appendix F.	25/10/1917	25/10/1917
Miscellaneous	125th Brigade. Appendix G.	27/10/1917	27/10/1917
Miscellaneous	Statement Shewing Strength Of Company, Casualties Etc. Appendix. H.	01/10/1917	01/10/1917
Heading	War Diary. for 125 Machine Gun Company. November 1st to November 30th 1917 Volume XI Vol 10		
War Diary	Belgium Map Ref. Furnes 1/40000 W18d55	01/11/1917	06/11/1917
War Diary	No. 5. 1/10000 Nieuport	07/11/1917	09/11/1917
War Diary	Belgium No 5 1/10000 Nieuport	10/11/1917	19/11/1917
War Diary	Dunkerque 1A 1/100000 Hazebrouck 1/100000	20/11/1917	23/11/1917
War Diary	France. Map. Ref Hazebrouck 1/100000	24/11/1917	28/11/1917

War Diary	Belgium Coubin Sheet. 1/40000	29/11/1917	30/11/1917
Miscellaneous	Relief Orders by Captain R V Gery, Commanding "Rain" Appendix A.	06/11/1917	06/11/1917
Operation(al) Order(s)	Operation Order No. 6. by Capt. G.C. Kay. Commanding 125th M.G. Company Appendix B.	18/11/1917	18/11/1917
Operation(al) Order(s)	Administrative Order To Accompany Operation Order No 6 Appendix B	13/11/1917	13/11/1917
Miscellaneous	Inter-Machine Gun Company Relief.	16/11/1917	16/11/1917
Miscellaneous	Inter-Machine Gun Company Relief	16/11/1917	16/11/1917
Map	Appendix B.		
Operation(al) Order(s)	125th Machine Gun Company. Order No. 8 By Captain G.C. Kay. Appendix C.	28/11/1917	28/11/1917
Miscellaneous	Relief Table:- Issued With M.G. Coy. to Order No.		
Miscellaneous	Administrative Order By Captain G.C. Kay. Commanding 125th M.G. Company		
Miscellaneous	Statement Shewing Strength Of Company, Casualties Ete. Appendix D.	01/11/1917	01/11/1917
Heading	War Diary for 125th Machine Gun Company. From December 1st to December 31st. 1917. Volume XII		
War Diary	France Map Ref. La Bassee 36c NW.1 1/10000	01/12/1917	10/12/1917
War Diary	36 A. SE 36 SW 36 & NE 36c NW Bethune Edt 6. 1/40000	11/12/1917	17/12/1917
War Diary	France Map Ref (36c SE 36 SW. 36b NE 36c N.W. Bethune Col 6 1/40000)	18/12/1917	19/12/1917
War Diary	36c N.W.1 La Bassee 1/10000 36 SW3 Ruche Bourg 1/10000	20/12/1917	24/12/1917
War Diary	France Ref Maps. 36c N.W.1 La Bassee 1/100000	25/12/1917	25/12/1917
War Diary	36 S.W.3. Riche Bourg 1/100000	26/12/1917	31/12/1917
Operation(al) Order(s)	Operation Order No. 9. by Captain G.C. Kay. Commanding 125th Machine Gun Company. Appendix A.	08/12/1917	08/12/1917
Operation(al) Order(s)	125 M.G. Coy. Administrative Instructions No. 9 To Accompany Operation Order No. 9 Appendix A.	08/12/1917	08/12/1917
Miscellaneous	Machine Gun Barrage Fire.	10/12/1917	10/12/1917
Operation(al) Order(s)	Operation Order No. 20. by Captain G.C. Kay Commanding 125th Machine Gun Company. Appendix B	21/12/1917	21/12/1917
Operation(al) Order(s)	Administrative Instructions by Captain G.C. Kay Issued With G.C. No. 10	21/12/1917	21/12/1917
Miscellaneous	Tactical and Technical Lessons Learnt During Month. Appendix C	21/12/1917	21/12/1917
Miscellaneous	Statement Shewing Strength of Company Casualties Etc. Appendix D		
Map	Identification Trace for use With Artillery Maps. Appendix E.		
Heading	War Diary for 125th Machine Gun Company From January 1st To January 31st 1918 Volume XIII		
War Diary	France Ref Maps 36c N.W1. La Bassee 1/10000	01/01/1918	01/01/1918
War Diary	36 S.W.3 Richebourg 1/10,000	02/01/1918	08/01/1918
War Diary	France Ref Maps 36c N.W.I. La Bassee 1/10000	08/01/1918	08/01/1918
War Diary	36. S.W.3 Richebourg 1/10000	08/01/1918	14/01/1918
War Diary	France Ref Maps 36c N.W.1 La Bassee 1/10000	15/01/1918	16/01/1918
War Diary	36 S.W.3 Richebourg 1/10000	16/01/1918	16/01/1918
War Diary	Richebourg 1/10000 36 A. SE. 36 S.W. 36 B. N.E. 36c NW.	17/01/1918	17/01/1918
War Diary	Bethune Edt 6 1/40000	18/01/1918	21/01/1918

War Diary	France Ref Maps. 36A SE 36 SW 36B NE 36c NW	22/01/1918	22/01/1918
War Diary	Bethune Edt. 6. 1/40000	23/01/1918	27/01/1918
War Diary	France Ref. Maps. 36A. SE 36 SW. 36 B.N.E. 36c N.W.	28/01/1918	28/01/1918
War Diary	Bethune Edt. 6 1/40000	29/01/1918	31/01/1918
Operation(al) Order(s)	Operation Order No. 14. By Captain G.C. Kay. Commanding 4 R.E. Appendix A	13/01/1918	13/01/1918
Operation(al) Order(s)	Operation Order No 15 Captain G.C. Kay Commanding 125th M.G Coy Appendix B.	28/01/1918	28/01/1918
Miscellaneous			
Miscellaneous	Tactical Technical Lessons Learnt During The Month Appendix C	17/01/1918	17/01/1918
Miscellaneous	Statement During Strength Of Company Casualties R.C. Appendix D		
Heading	War Diary for 125th Machine Gun Company From February 1st To February 28th 1918 Volume XIV Vol 13		
War Diary	France Ref. Maps 1/10000 36c NW 1	01/02/1918	01/02/1918
War Diary	La Bassee & 1/40000 36 A. S.E. 36 S W. 36 B.N.E. 36. C.N.W.	02/02/1918	03/02/1918
War Diary	Bethune	04/02/1918	10/02/1918
War Diary	France Ref. Map. 1/10000 36c NW1 La Bassee	11/02/1918	14/02/1918
War Diary	1/40000 36A S.E. 36 S.W. 3C B.W.E. 36C. N.W.	15/02/1918	18/02/1918
War Diary	France Ref Maps 1/40000 36 A.S.E. 36. S.W. 36 B.NE. 36c N.W.	19/02/1918	25/02/1918
War Diary	France Ref Maps. 1/40000 36A. SE. 36.B.N.W. 36. B.N.E.	26/02/1918	28/02/1918
Operation(al) Order(s)	Operation Order No. 16 by Capt. G.C. Kay. Commanding 125th Machine Gun Company Appendix A.	12/02/1918	12/02/1918
Miscellaneous	March and Relief Table to accompany 125 M.G. Coy. Operation Order No. 16		
Operation(al) Order(s)	125th Machine Gun Company Administrative Instruction No16. Issued in Inspection With O.O. 16 Appendix	12/02/1918	12/02/1918
Miscellaneous	125th M.G. Coy. Reinforcement Scheme. Appendix B	27/02/1918	27/02/1918
Miscellaneous	After Order.	25/02/1918	25/02/1918
Miscellaneous	O.E. 125 M.G. Coy.		
Miscellaneous	Tactical and Technical Lessons Learnt During The Month	20/02/1918	20/02/1918
Miscellaneous	Statement Shewing Strength of Company Casualties Etc. Appendix D	28/02/1918	28/02/1918
Miscellaneous	Fire Calculations	06/02/1918	06/02/1918
Miscellaneous	Fire Casualties.	06/02/1918	06/02/1918
Map	Map		

WO95/2655-3

125 Bde MG Coy — 42 Div

Mar 1917 – Feb 1918

42ND DIVISION
125TH INFY BDE.

125TH MACHINE GUN COY.
MAR 1917-FEB 1918

CONFIDENTIAL.

Vol 2

WAR DIARY
of
the 125th MACHINE GUN Coy.

from March 1st 1917 to March 31st 1917.

(Volume III.)

Mar 17
Feb 18

WAR DIARY

~~INTELLIGENCE SUMMARY~~
(Erase heading not required.)

Army Form C. 2118

125 COMPANY MACHINE GUN CORPS
MARCH 1917.

Place	Date 1917.	Hour	Summary of Events and Information	Remarks and references to Appendices
FRANCE MAÇON	March 1	0730	Arrived MAÇON. Stopped 45 minutes for breakfast.	
		1500	Arrived LES LAUMES - ALÉSIA. Stopped 1¼ hours for dinners.	
		2115	Arrived MONTEREAU. Stopped 1¼ hours for tea.	
	2	1030	Arrived EPLUCHES. Stopped 1 hour for a meal.	
PONT RÉMY		1730	Arrived PONT RÉMY; detrained. Company, less 2/Lt. R.E.F. BARNETT & 23 O.R. detached to take over transport, marched to CHÂTEAU VIEULAINE, distance 5 miles.	Appx.
Ref. Maps Fourth Army Area Colomber Directors Map March 2. Scale 1:100000		2015	Arrived CHÂTEAU VIEULAINE & billetted there for night.	Appx.
FONTAINE-SUR-SOMME	3	2145	Company employed on fatigues & cleaning up. Evacuated billets at CHÂTEAU VIEULAINE marched to FONTAINE-SUR-SOMME (1 mile) billetted in empty barns.	Appendix I Sketch & billetting area. Appx.
		1415		
	4		Company employed digging latrines, fatigues etc. 2/LIEUT. R.W. LUCAS & 40 O.R. with 10 officers chargers rejoined, having left 1 O.R. in hospital at MARSEILLES.	Appx.
	5	2100	Physical Training.	
		0700	Route march to PONT RÉMY Stack, distance covered 7 miles.	
		0900	Equipping. 2/LIEUT. R.E.F. BARNETT & 23 O.R. rejoined, having 46 vehicles from Remount Depôt, ABBEVILLE	Appx.
"	6	1400	Physical Training.	
		0700	Route march to SOREL without transport. distance covered 5 miles, under LIEUT. G.S. WAREHAM	
		0900	Lecture Trench Warfare by certain officers.	
"	7	1400	Physical Training.	
		0700	Route march under LIEUT. G.S. WAREHAM to CORVEREL, distances covered 4 miles without transport	Appx.
		0900		

Army Form C. 2118

125th COMPANY
MACHINE GUN CORPS
MARCH 1917.

WAR DIARY
or
INTELLIGENCE SUMMARY
(Erase heading not required.)

Instructions regarding War Diaries and Intelligence Summaries are contained in F. S. Regs., Part II. and the Staff Manual respectively. Title Pages will be prepared in manuscript.

Place	Date 1917	Hour	Summary of Events and Information	Remarks and references to Appendices
FRANCE FONTAINE Ref. Maps Fourth Army Area Administrative Instruction Impt. Sheets 2 Scale 1:100,000	March 7	1100	Equipping. Lecture on 'Trench Warfare' by Section Officers	J.M.
		1400	Physical Training.	
	8	0700	Kit Inspections by Section Officers	J.M.
		0900	Squad Drill under Section Officers.	
		1400	Physical Training.	
	9	0700	Route march via PONT RÉMY to SOREL to FONTAINE under LIEUT. G.S. WAREHAM, distance covered 7½ miles in 2½ hours.	J.M.
FONTAINE-SUR-SOMME.		0900	Lectures on 'Trench Warfare' by Section Officers.	
		1400	Drew 16 Vickers Guns & Tripods Complete Spare Parts, Belt Ammunition Boxes from D.A.D.O.S. PONT RÉMY.	N.M.
"	10	0700	Physical Training.	
		0900	Guns & equipment issued to Sections. 1 O.R. to 3rd Army Corps School for duty	J.M.
			Anti gas equipment Steel helmets drawn from Ordnance PONT RÉMY	
"	11	0900	Church Parades. 1 O.R. proceeded to 4th Army Anti-gas School at PONT NOYELLES for instruction.	
			1 O.R. Joined 125th Coy. 429th Supply Column 429th Coy. A.S.C. at FONTAINE for duty.	
			Further machine gun parts drawn from Ordnance PONT RÉMY.	J.M.
"	12	0700	Spare M.G. & equipment issued Sections.	
		0900	Company Route march under Capt. B. LOWE with Transport to PONT RÉMY distance covered 6½ miles.	

Army Form C. 2118.

WAR DIARY
or
INTELLIGENCE SUMMARY.
(Erase heading not required.)

125th COMPANY
MACHINE GUN CORPS
MARCH 1917.

Place	Date 1917.	Hour	Summary of Events and Information	Remarks and references to Appendices
FONTAINE- SUR-SOMME	March 12	1400	Instruction on Vickers Guns for Officers & N.C.O's. Bren rifles & bayonets for attached men.	
Ref. Map French Army Gen: Admin. Wireless Ref. Sheet 2.	" 13		Anniversary of formation of Company.	
		0900	All Officers & N.C.O.'s fired 2 Vickers gun tests.	
Scale 1:100000	" 14	1400	New Vickers gun issued, fired on 30 yds. range near FONTAINE. Fired well.	
		0645	Drew 16 sets of Hackenberg & 4 bicycles from Ordnance PONT REMY.	
		0900	Steel helmets issued to section & rifles to attached men.	
			Baggage loading fatigue.	
			Lieut. G.S. WAREHAM & 2 O.R. proceeded by road to HAMEL as Billeting & ration Party.	* Appendix II Extracts from Operation Order 26.
	" 15		* Lieut. R.W. LUCAS LUCAS & 31 O.R. with Transport proceeded by road to HAMEL. Company's equipment, stores & Baggage to HAMEL. Both parties billeted for the night of the 14-15- at ST. SAUVEUR.	
		1600	Lieut. R. ALDERSON & 12 O.R. (Traffic Control Party) were attached to the Company.	
		0900	* Evacuated billets at FONTAINE-SUR-SOMME & marched to LONGPRES. 6 Officers & 116 O.R. entrained at LONGPRES.	* Appendix III. Operation Order 27.
		1030	Lieut. J.F. LARKINS & 1 O.R. was left behind as Rear Party. 2 O.R. proceeded to ABBEVILLE to obtain 1 G.S. limbered wagon & 2 light draught horses to complete establishment.	
		1130	Train left LONGPRES.	
CORBIE Ref. Map 1:40,000 Sheet 62 at 1:1 Scale 100000		1345	Arrived at CORBIE & detrained. Marched to HAMEL via FOUILLOY, HAMELET, VAIRE; distance 5 miles.	

Army Form C. 2118.

125 COMPANY
MACHINE GUN CORPS.
MARCH 1917.

WAR DIARY
or
INTELLIGENCE SUMMARY.
(Erase heading not required.)

Instructions regarding War Diaries and Intelligence Summaries are contained in F.S. Regs., Part II and the Staff Manual respectively. Title pages will be prepared in manuscript.

Place	Date 1917.	Hour	Summary of Events and Information	Remarks and references to Appendices
FRANCE. HAMEL.	March 15	1730	Arrived at HAMEL. * Officers were billetted at Troines in the RUE DE CORBIE & the remainder Other Company & Transport at 175 Troines.	* Appendix II. Photo of billeting Area.
Ref. Map Sheet 62 D Ed. 1. Scale 40000 P.18.a.	16	0900	Fatigues & cleaning up billets. 33 O.R. arrived from Training Gun Corps Base Depot, CAMIERS completing the establishment of the Company to 177 O.R. LIEUT. D.F. LARKINS & 1 O.R. rejoined.	J.McK.
		1600	Drew picketting gear from III. Corps Ordnance WARFUSEE.	J.McK.
"	17	0900	Cleaning guns & gun equipment, harness etc.	
		1030	2 O.R. arrived with 1 G.S. Limbered wagon & 2 lifts draught horses.	J.McK.
"	18	0945	CAPT. B. LOWE & 2 O.R. proceeded to the 1st Division in the Trenches for 48 hours for instruction. LIEUT. G.C. KAY assumed the Company during the absence of CAPT. B. LOWE.	
		1150	Drew miscellaneous stores from A.O.D. WARFUSEE.	J.McK.
		1430	Church Parade.	
"	19	0700	Physical Training.	
		0900 to 1215	Tactical exercises & Gun Drill.	
		1400 to 1600	do. do.	J.McK.

Army Form C. 2118.

125 COMPANY,
MACHINE GUN CORPS.
MARCH. 1917.

WAR DIARY
INTELLIGENCE SUMMARY.
(Erase heading not required.)

Instructions regarding War Diaries and Intelligence Summaries are contained in F. S. Regs., Part II. and the Staff Manual respectively. Title pages will be prepared in manuscript.

Place	Date 1917.	Hour	Summary of Events and Information	Remarks and references to Appendices
FRANCE. HAMEL Ref. Map Sheet 62.3 ed. I. Scale 1:40,000 P.10.a.	March 20	0700	Physical Training.	
		0900 to 11.45	Mobile march under LIEUT. G.S. WAREHAM along CERISY road to WARFUSÉE. Track; distance covered 7 miles. Foot inspection.	
		1400 to 15.45	Lecture on "Trench WARFARE"; Gun cleaning; Gun lecture by Div: Gas Officer. Capt. B. LOWE T 2.O.R. returned from instructional Town walk. 2/Lt. M.G. C. & Lieut. G.C. KAY T 2.O.R. proceeded to 2nd Battn. M.G. Co. for the same purpose. Capt. J. LOWE resumed command of the Company.	M.C.
"	21	0900 to 1200	Gun Drill, Inclinometer, Stoppages.	
		1400 to 1600	Lectures, Indicator, Recognition of Targets.	M.C.
"	22	0900 to 11.45	Section drill by C.O. Open Warfare. Extended order dressing.	
		1400 to 1600	Inclinometer, Stoppages.	
"	23	0900 to 1.15	LIEUT. G.C. KAY T 2.O.R. returned from instructional Town. 2 LIEUT. HERRIDGE, A.L. assumed command of the Transport in place of LIEUT. R.W. LUCAS. LUCAS.	M.C.
		1400 to 1600	Route march under LIEUT. G.S. WAREHAM to HAMELET via VAIRE, distance covered 6 miles.	
		1600 to 1500	Lecture on Discipline by Acting Officer C.O. Gun cleaning. Officer theoretical examinent from Ordnance under C.O. WARFUSÉE.	M.C.
"	24	0900 to 1100	Drew fourteen rifts from Ordnance WARFUSÉE. Cleaning kit & Equipt issued. C.O's Inspection.	M.C.

2353 Wt. W2544/1454 700,000 5/15 D.D.& L. A.D.S.S./Form/C. 2118.

Army Form C. 2118.

WAR DIARY
or
~~INTELLIGENCE SUMMARY~~
(Erase heading not required.)

125 COMPANY,
MACHINE GUN CORPS,
MARCH 1917.

Instructions regarding War Diaries and Intelligence Summaries are contained in F. S. Regs, Part II. and the Staff Manual respectively. Title pages will be prepared in manuscript.

Place	Date 1917.	Hour.	Summary of Events and Information	Remarks and references to Appendices
FRANCE. HAMEL Ref. Map Sheet 62d col 1. Scale 1/40000 P.10.a.	March 25	a.m.	The 125 Brigade turned by route march to ECLUSIER, FRISE & FEUILLERES via CERISY, MERICOURT, FROISSY.	× Appendix 1 Sketch of billets
		7.0	The Company evacuated billets at HAMEL. LIEUT. G.S. WAREHAM preceded the Company as billetting Officer.	
		7.20	Company turned off with transport, guns Stores, 8 Officers & 195 O.R. 6 O.R. proceeded by motor lorry with baggage & blankets. Position on line of march between 6: L.F. & 7: L.F.	
		12.30	Halted for 1 hour for dinners ½ mile S.W. of CAPPY.	
FRISE Sheet 62c col 1. Scale 1/40000 G.18.d.		p.m. 3.30	Arrived at FRISE. Company billetted in dug-outs & tents empty horse vard Church west side. One light draught horse fell ill & died from unknown causes at commencement of march. Certificate of Veterinary Officer obtained. 2 O.R. fell out on march. Capt. B. LOWE proceeded to M.G.T.C. GRANTHAM for a Course of Instruction. LIEUT. G.E. KAY assumed command of the Company in Capt. B. LOWE's place. One O.R. proceeded to U.K. on 10 days furlough.	
	26 All day		Clearing billetting area; gun & equipment inspection. 10 O.R. admitted Battsfield. (lying sick, not on duty.) Cleaning inspection of guns. 10 G.S. limbered wagons supplied to 5: L.F. Kit Inspections by Section Officers.	
	27	a.m. 9.0 10.0 12.15 p.m. 2.0 3.0 6.0	Saluting drill. Luncheon. N.O.'s Inspection. 10 cases of Scabies. This would appear to be a recurrence of outbreak at EL ARISH. One O.R. proceeded to U.K. on 10 days furlough. LIEUT. H.B. CARLISLE proceeded to M.G.C. Base School for a Course of Instruction at CAMIERS.	

2353 Wt. W3511/1454 700,000 5/15 D.D.&L. A.D.S.S./Form/C. 2118.

Army Form C. 2118.

125 COMPANY,
MACHINE GUN CORPS,
MARCH 1917.

WAR DIARY
or
INTELLIGENCE SUMMARY.
(Erase heading not required.)

Instructions regarding War Diaries and Intelligence Summaries are contained in F. S. Regs., Part II. and the Staff Manual respectively. Title pages will be prepared in manuscript.

Place	Date 1917.	Hour	Summary of Events and Information	Remarks and references to Appendices
FRANCE	March 28	a.m. 6.45	3 Officer & 115 O.R. with 1 G.S. limbered wagon with cook travelling marched to BIACHES as a working party for road mending.	
Ref. Map Trench 62c ed 11. Scale 1/40000 G.18.d.		8.30	10 G.S. limbered wagons supplied for clearing station for Brigade. 3 O.R. sent to Field Ambulance (scabies, general scarlet, neuritis.)	J.H.C.
		p.m. 6.0	Working party returned.	
	29	a.m. 6.45	Working party as yesterday & 3 Officer & 108 O.R. to BIACHES. Working party G.S. limbered wagons sent to each cache etc.	
		to 6.0	LIEUT. M.A.S. BREDSFORD proceeded to U.K. on 10 days leave. 1 O.R. returned from hospital.	J.H.C.
	30	a.m. 9.0 to 12.15	Mothers' Parade for washing clothes under section arrangements. 6 G.S. limbered wagons supplied for working parties.	
		p.m. 2.0 to 4.0	Equipping exchange of clothing by gun. Clearing from & guidewind. 3 O.R. to Field Ambulance (rheumatism, scabies, septic leg.)	J.H.C.
	31	a.m. 6.45 to p.m. 5.45	Working party 3 Officer & 98 O.R. to BIACHES. All limbers supplied for working parties etc. 6 L.D. horses with harness sent to AMIEN's with 3 drivers. 1 O.R. rejoined from hospital.	J.H.C.

Very Very
31/3/17

Appendix I.

RF = 1/7920

FONTAINE-S-SOMME

EACH SQUARE = 1"
8" = 1 mile   1" = 220 yds

B.M = BOUNDARY MARK.

Appendix II. Extracts from Operation Order 26.

Secret.

Reference Map 1: 100,000. Sheet ABBEVILLE. 14.
125th Machine Gun Company. Order no 26.
In the Field.
March 13th 1917.

1. The 125th Machine Gun Company will move from HALLENCOURT AREA to HAMEL on the 14th & 15th inst.
    Transport 14th inst.
    Remainder 15th inst.

2. Transport will move by March Route via PICQUINY, RILLY-SUR-SOMME, ST. SAUVEUR, ARGUEVUES, AMMES, LONGEAU, BLANGY-TRONVILLE, FOUILLOY, HAMELET, VAIRE, & HAMEL. This party will take one day's rations & will be under the O.C. 429th Company A.S.C.

3. The position on the line of march for tomorrow is between 8th L.F. & 429th Coy. R.E.

4. LIEUT. G.S. WAREHAM & Serjt. TURNER, W.G. (both mounted) will precede the Transport column & find billets for the Transport party for night 14th/15th inst. at ST. SAUVEUR and ARGUVUES & for the Transport column and the remainder of their Units for the nights of the 15th/16th at HAMEL. They will also arrange billets for 13th K.G. They will have complete information as to the strength of their parties.

5. Billeting party will report to O.C. 429th Coy. A.S.C. at rendezvous at 1000 on the 14th inst.

6. Supplies will be drawn at WARFUSEE-ABANCOURT on the 15th for the 16th.

7. Transport vehicles will travel with their proper loads. Arrangements for the moving of baggage & stores will be made later.

8. March discipline must be strictly enforced.

9. Transport will rendezvous at LONGPRES at 1015 & will report arrival to O.C. 429th Coy. A.S.C.

10. Remainder of Company will entrain at LONGPRES & detrain at CORBIE on the 15th inst. Time of departure of train will be notified later.

11. Stores which cannot be taken in transport will be conveyed to the dump either at LIERCOURT or PONT REMY. After unloading baggage for the dump the lorries will proceed with the remainder of the load to FOUILLOY.

12. ~~The dump will jfk.~~ . . . . .

Signed
Bertram Lowe Capt.
Commanding 125 Machine Gun Co.

Issued at 1805. by Orderly.

Appendix 3.

Copy No.....

125th. Machine Gun Company.   Order N° 27.

Ref. Map. 1/100,000 ABBEVILLE.

In the Field.
14th. March. 1917.

1. The Company will entrain at LONGPRE to-morrow on N° 1. Train which leaves at 1100. Time to be at station ready for entraining 1015. The following troops will proceed by this train:-

   | | Off. | O.R. |
   125th Machine Gun Company.   5.   126.
   also Brigade H.Q., 8th L.F., 5th L.F., and 427 Field Coy, R.E.
   O.C. train is Lieut. Col. O. St. L. Davies. 8th. L.F.

2. The Company will parade in full marching order ready to move off from N° 2 BILLET ECHOLE DES GARSONS by 0830.

3. The following route will be followed:-
   FONTAINE - VIEULAINE - LONGPRE.

4. Care will be taken to leave all Billets in a clean and tidy condition. All latrines and pits filled in and marked and all rubbish disposed of.

5. The following rear party will be left behind:-
   =LIEUT. D.F. LARKINS 39602 PTE. GARSTANG G.C.
   This party to take two days rations and will be attached to Brigade Salvage Corps under 2nd LIEUT. BREMNER. at LIERCOURT., and proceed to HAMEL by motor lorry on the 16th inst.

6. All cyclists of the Brigade group will rendezvous on the road EAST of LONGPRE station at 1130 on the 15th inst., and proceed under the command of an officer to be detailed by O.C. 5th. L.F. to ST. SAUVEUR This party will billet at ST. SAUVEUR on the night of the 15th/16th. inst., and proceed to HAMEL on the 16th inst.,

(signed) Bertram Lowe.
Captain.
Commanding 125th Machine Gun Company.

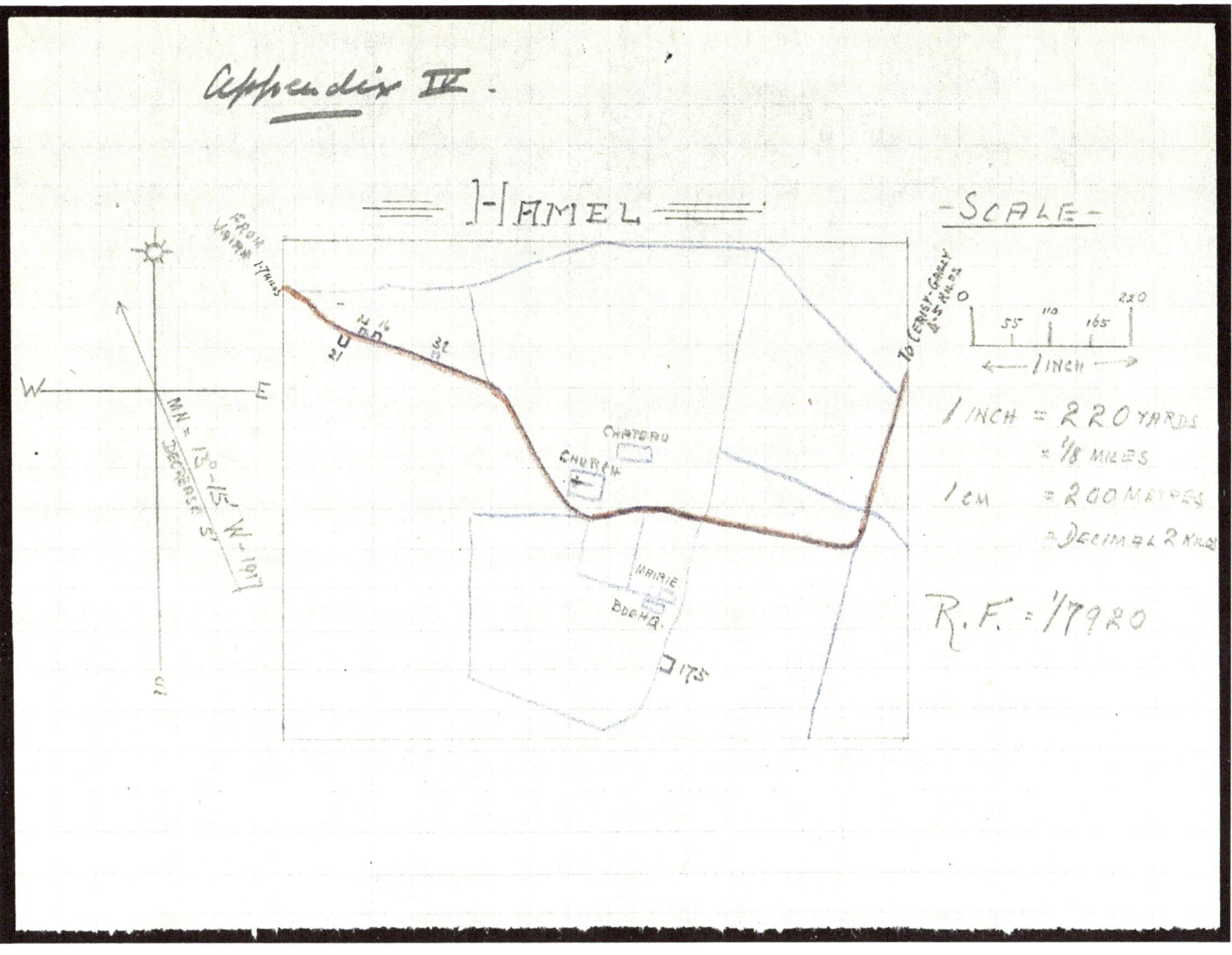

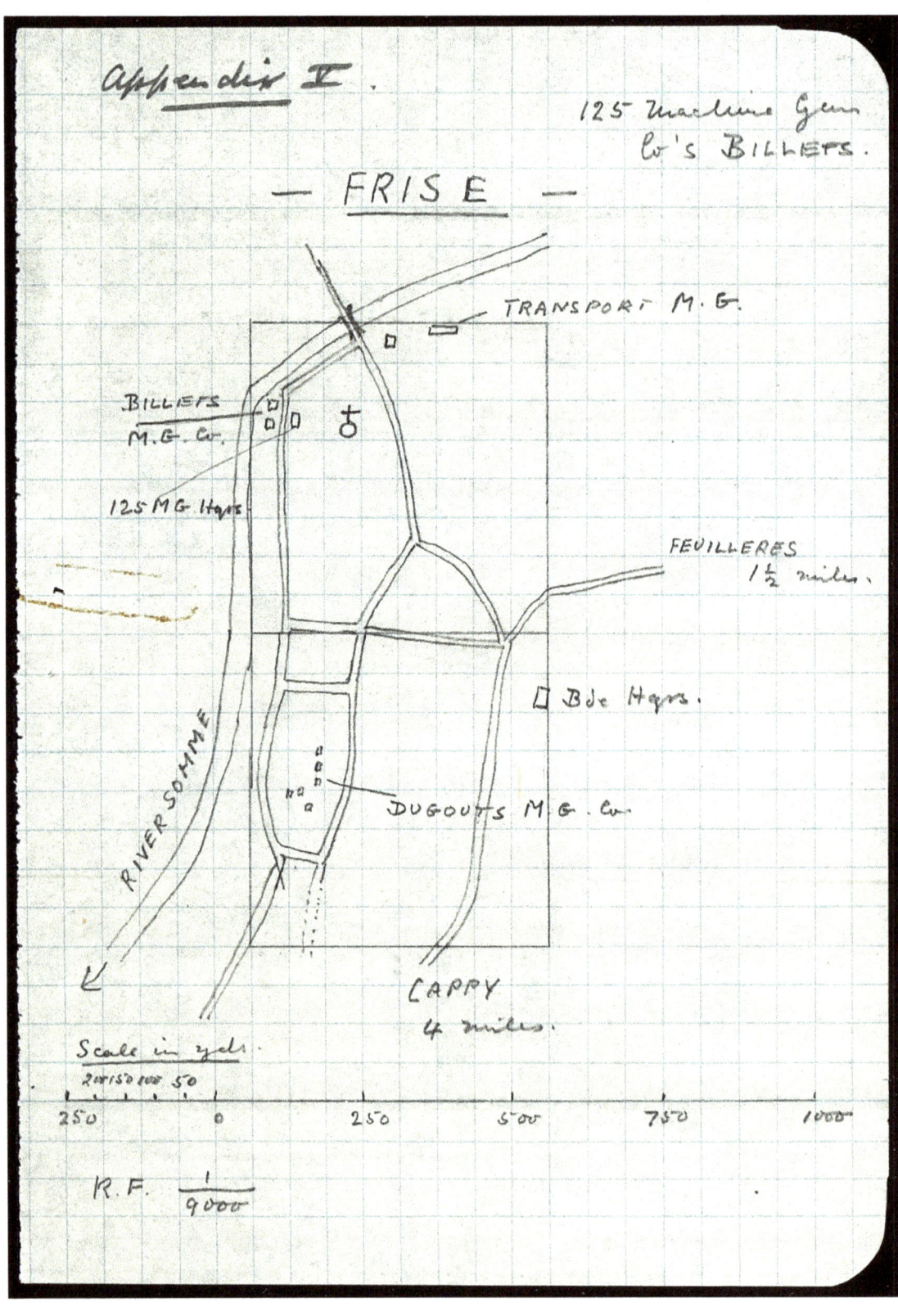

CONFIDENTIAL.

Vol 3

War Diary
of
the 125th Machine Gun Coy

from April 1st 1917 to April 30th 1917.

(Volume IV.)

Army Form C. 2118.

125 COMPANY,
MACHINE GUN CORPS,
APRIL 1917.

WAR DIARY
or
INTELLIGENCE SUMMARY
(Erase heading not required.)

Instructions regarding War Diaries and Intelligence Summaries are contained in F.S. Regs., Part II. and the Staff Manual respectively. Title pages will be prepared in manuscript.

Place	Date 1917.	Hour	Summary of Events and Information	Remarks and references to Appendices
FRANCE.	April 1		Capt. N.V. GERY 4th: City of London M.G.C. was taken on the strength of the Company. Total over war need or turned 31st 1917:	
FRISE		a.m.	Working party 3 Officers & 90 O.R. G.J. ACHES engaged for	
Ref. Trench		6.45	carrying stores. 6 O.R. in Hospital stores off the strength of Company.	
Sheet 62c				
od 1.		6.30 p.m.	2/Lieut. N.F. SMITH returned from leave in the U.K.	
Scale 1/40000			1 O.R. went to Field Ambulance (Diarrhoea)	
G.18.d.			1 O.R. proceeded to U.K. on 10 days furlough.	
	2	a.m.	Working party 2 Officers & 70 O.R. to HERBECOURT, 6 Limbers for carting	N.R.
		7.15	materials. Remainder of Coy on fatigues.	
			1 O.R. to Field Ambulance (septic sores)	
		6.30 p.m.	1 O.R. returned from Field Ambulance.	
	3	a.m.	Working party 2 Officers & 54 O.R. to HERBECOURT with 6 Limbers	N.R.
		7.20	Remainder of Coy. gas drill.	
		10.20 a.m.	Instruction on gas.	
		2.0 p.m.	Lieut. H.B. CARLISLE reported from CAMIERS.	N.R.
		4.0	Working party 3 Officers & 102 O.R. to HERBECOURT, & 6 Limbers.	
	4	7.20	Three men cleaning guns etc.	
			2 O.R. went to Hospital (influenza, scabies)	
			returned from Hospital.	
			9 O.R.	
	5	a.m.	Working party 3 Officers & 105 O.R. to HERBECOURT & 6 Limbers.	N.R.
		7.20	1 O.R. returned from Field Ambulance.	
		6.30 p.m.		
	6	a.m.	Working party 3 Officers & 110 O.R. to HERBECOURT & 2 Limbers.	
		7.20	2 Limbers removed 125 Coy baggage to PERONNE.	
		10.30	(Three Limbers are employed daily drawing rations for Company & French Trench Battery.)	

Army Form C. 2118.

125 COMPANY,
MACHINE GUN CORPS,
APRIL 1917.

WAR DIARY
or
INTELLIGENCE SUMMARY.
(Erase heading not required.)

Instructions regarding War Diaries and Intelligence Summaries are contained in F. S. Regs., Part II. and the Staff Manual respectively. Title pages will be prepared in manuscript.

Place	Date 1917.	Hour	Summary of Events and Information	Remarks and references to Appendices
Peronne.	March 7	6.30 a.m.	1.O.R. returned from Hospital.	HH.
		7.0	Fatigues, cleaning billets, fatiguing trenches.	
		9.0	Capt. G.S. WAREHAM & 1.O.R. proceeded to PERONNE on billetting party.	
Ref. Map. 62c Sud. Scale 40000		12.30	The Company marched to PERONNE with transport via FEUILLERS, HEM, CLERY. 6.O.R. were left behind in charge of 3 lorries with guns etc. of 2nd 1 section stores.	
I. 27. 4. 8. 6	8	4.0 a.m.	Company reached PERONNE and billetted in cellars etc.	HH.
		3.30 a.m.	Nothing doing.	
		7.30 to 6 p.m.	Working party & Officers & 101 O.R. to DOINGT. 2 limbers & 3 extra teams sent to FRISE for missing limbers & stores.	
			1.O.R. returned from Hospital. 1.O.R. proceeded to V.R. on 10 days furlough. 1.O.R.	
	9	6.30 to 10.30	The Company with transport, less 3 limbers left behind, travelled, marched by road to LONGAVESNES via BUSSU.	HH.
E. 25. F. 2. B.		12.50	Arrived LONGAVESNES & bivouaced for the night. 1.O.R. returned from furlough. 3 O.R. went to Field Ambulance.	
	10	6.30 a.m.	Machine Guns & cleaning guns.	
		9.0	The Company relieved the 143rd W. Yorkshire Gun Company in the front line. X	X Appendix I. General Sit-
Ref. Map 62c N.E. scale 20000 F. l. a. 5.		9.0 p.m. 9.0	1.O.R. returned from Hospital.	uation & positions of guns.
	11		EPEHY & surrounding villages shelled intermittently by enemy. No action on front of our machine guns. No enemy sighted.	
		9 a.m. 2 p.m.	Gas instruction for men at Hqrs. Weather: strong westerly wind, cold, fine, falling at night, snow. 1.O.R. returned from furlough. 2.O.R. proceeded on 10 days furlough.	HH.
	12	9 a.m.	Situation in previous day's Headquarters. Gas lectures for men at Headquarters. 1.O.R. work on furlough. LIEUT. M.A.S. BRESSFORD returned from leave.	

Army Form C. 2118.

WAR DIARY
~~INTELLIGENCE~~ SUMMARY
(Erase heading not required.)

**125 COMPANY,
MACHINE GUN CORPS.
APRIL 1917.**

Instructions regarding War Diaries and Intelligence Summaries are contained in F.S. Regs., Part II. and the Staff Manual respectively. Title pages will be prepared in manuscript.

Place	Date 1917.	Hour	Summary of Events and Information	Remarks and references to Appendices
FRANCE. Ref. Trench Map 57^c S.E. 62.c N.E. 1 Scale 20000	April 12 13	4 a.m. 9.0	125 Brigade seized line Opus no 12 - X.27.a.4.1. This was successfully accomplished by 10 a.m. without serious opposition. The guns in the right sector were sited for indirect fire, to support the infantry on F.4 & 05.72. Two machine guns in either sector were required to fire front Pay received in their original position. Enemy artillery active during shellng railway cutting in front of EPEHY with H.E. & various types. The enemy observed, situation quiet during the day. 1 O.R. was to field ambulance (Rheumatism) 1 2 O.R. proceeded on 10 days furlough witnesses to Railway.	THC.
		8 p.m.	No 3 gun moved 25 yards right, situation nil to enemy shelling.	THC.
	April 14	4 a.m. 7.20	1 new Vickers gun brought back by order of V.O. came debility. Situation in machine gun front unchanged. No enemy visible. Intermittent artillery on our front. Photo of this enemy. Quick day. Enemy aeroplane active 7 & 8 a.m.	
		7 a.m.	3 enemy aeroplanes seen through anti-aircraft barrage in direction of PERONNE. One of our observation balloons set on fire. Pay returned again in about 15 minutes.	
		5. O.R.	proceeded to PERONNE with 9 sick horses.	
			LIEUT. A.L. HERRIDGE T. I.O.R. proceeded on 10 days leave.	THC.
	15	a.m. 7.20	Situation quiet in right sector throughout the day. Target escaped for intermittent shelling on both sides.	
		9 a.m.	An enemy aeroplane attacked our observation balloon in flames by guns fire, after dividing the right sector but was driven off by gun fire. No 143 Inf. Machine Gun Co. No. 254 the Company was relieved by 2 Zealand & carried at 9 p.m. section in the line were relieved at 9 p.m. for the remainder of this night.	THC.
LONGAVESNES		9.30	by 8.30 a.m. Strength of Company at this date 10 Officers 177 O.R	THC.

2353 Wt. W 2514/1454. 700,000 5/15. D.D.&L. A.D.S.S./Forms/C. 2118.

Army Form C. 2118.

WAR DIARY
or
INTELLIGENCE SUMMARY.
(Erase heading not required.)

**125 MACHINE GUN COMPANY,
MACHINE GUN CORPS,
APRIL 1917.**

Instructions regarding War Diaries and Intelligence Summaries are contained in F. S. Regs., Part II. and the Staff Manual respectively. Title pages will be prepared in manuscript.

Place	Date 1917.	Hour	Summary of Events and Information	Remarks and references to Appendices
FRANCE. Ref. Trench. April/16 57c S.E. 62c N.E. scale 1/20000 Ref. Trench. 62c 1/40000	April 16	night.	The Company proceeded to PERONNE by route march & billetted there for the night. Nos. 1 & 3 Sections, fighting strength arriving at 2.6.30. p.m. Nos. 2 & 4 arriving 5 h.m. The remainder of the Company arriving at 1.30 h.m. 3 limbers were left behind loaded as 4 extra limbers were provided by Brigade for transporting stores. 3 limbers were left behind loaded as the horses were sick.	
	17	7.m. 12.15	The Company proceeded by route march to FRISE carrying first a water tong supply waggon provided for transport. Reps. was billetted at G.15.d.6.3, Transport at G.18.c.7.7.1. at G.11.d.9.3. returned from leave. 2 O.R. admitted to Field Ambulance. 2 O.R. returned from leave.	
	18	6.m. 9.0 12.0 1.m. 2.0	Cleaning guns, equipment etc. The Company tactical at FRISE baths. 2.O.R. proceeded on 10 days leave. 1.O.R. struck off strength, evacuated to Fienvillers.	
	19	a.m. 9.0 12.0 2.0 4.30	Elementary gun drill, firing on 30° range, instructional. Marched to CAPPY for tactical schemes of inclusion & immediate action. Nos. 3 & 4 sections worked army to & case of Trenches. Nos. 3 & 4 sections worked army to & case of Trenches. 3 limbers & 3 spare horses sent to PERONNE for trenches stores left behind.	
	20	a.m. 9.0 12.0	1.O.R. went on leave. 3.O.R. admitted to Field Ambulance. 1.O.R. returned from Field Ambulance. Nos. 1 & 2 Sections exchange of clothing & equipment; immediate action. Nos. 3 & 4 Sections firing set off range.	

Army Form C. 2118.

WAR DIARY
or
INTELLIGENCE SUMMARY.
(Erase heading not required.)

125th COMPANY,
MACHINE GUN CORPS.
APRIL 1917.

Instructions regarding War Diaries and Intelligence Summaries are contained in F.S. Regs., Part II. and the Staff Manual respectively. Title pages will be prepared in manuscript.

Place	Date 1917.	Hour	Summary of Events and Information	Remarks and references to Appendices
Infy. Dugts. 62c	April 20	2.0 p.m.	Squad drills in respirators, gun drills etc.	
		4.0	4. O.R. proceeded on leave. 5 O.R. attached were returned to their units	
FRISE			6 LAN. FUS. under Brigade instructions.	
	21	9 a.m.	3/4 section marched to CAPPY for bath & change of underclothing.	
		7.0	1/2 section bath and stoppages.	
		9.0 a	Washing, packing & Limbers.	
		6.30	1 sick horse died of Enteritis.	
		2.0 G	Men seen by V.O.	
		4.0	4. O.R. proceeded on leave. 1. O.R. admitted to Field Ambulance. The	
	22	4.30	Company moved by route march from FRISE to PERONNE	Rickets I.27. to 48.
		9.30	arriving at 1.15 p.m. 3 Limbers were left behind as the horses were sick	
			with a guard of 4 O.R. 2 O.R. attached to 16.44 Sick Horse Lines in	
			Lestation. 3. O.R. proceeded on leave. 3 O.R. returned from Leave.	
			1. O.R. returned from hospital. 1. O.R. returned from Leave.	
PERONNE			Strength of Company at this date 10 Officers & 164 O.R.	
	23	9 a.m.	Washing harness 2 Officers & 60 O.R. cleaning vehicles.	The
		8.30	No 1 section gun drill & immediate action.	
		12.0		
		2.05	No 1 section rough ground drill, drill in gas respirators.	
		5.0	1. O.R. returned from hospital. 4 O.R. went on leave.	
	24	9 a.m.	Washing harn 2 Officers & 70 O.R.	Etc.
		8.30	No 2 section loading Limbers with Munitions, inclinometer rough ground drill.	
		12.0		
		2.0 G	Immediate action, care & cleaning, mortise range practice.	
		5.0	4. O.R. went on leave. 1. O.R. Hospital (scabies) Medical Inspection of Company. 9/6	
		6.30	5. O.R. attached returned to their Units, 3 to 5 LAN. FUS. 2 to 8 LAN. FUS.	

2353. Wt. W2341/1454 700,000 5/15 D.D.&L. A.D.S.S./Form/C. 2118.

Army Form C. 2118.

WAR DIARY
~~INTELLIGENCE SUMMARY~~
(Erase heading not required.)

125 COMPANY,
MACHINE GUN CORPS.
APRIL 1917.

Instructions regarding War Diaries and Intelligence Summaries are contained in F. S. Regs., Part II. and the Staff Manual respectively. Title pages will be prepared in manuscript.

Place	Date 1917.	Hour	Summary of Events and Information	Remarks and references to Appendices
FRANCE Ref. Map 62c 1/40000 PERONNE I.27.6.	April 25	6 a.m. 8.15 6.12.0 2.0 G 4.0	Working Party 2 Officers & 60 O.R. 2nd 3 section in musketry orders; 1 mag. ground drill. 2nd 3 section firing stoppages. 7.O.R. went on leave. 3 O.R. returned from leave. 1 O.R. rejoined from Field Ambulance. 1 O.R. joined from Machine Gun Base.	J.H.
"	26	6 a.m. 8.15 12.0 2.0 G 4.30 p.m.	Working Party 2 Officers & 55 men. 2nd 4 section firing on 30x range. Fired German gun. 2nd 4 section fired stoppages. 4 O.R. went on leave.	J.H.
"	27	6 a.m. 8.15 12.0 2.0 P 4.30 p.m.	Working Party 1 Officer & 49 O.R. 2nd 1 section firing on 30x range. Fired German gun. 2nd 1 section fired stoppages. 1 N.C.O. forwarded to Transport course. Record Depot, ABBEVILLE. LIEUT. H.B. CARLISLE & 1 Trumpeter & 2 N.C.Os. forwarded Stationary Gun School, CAMIERS for a course of instruction. 4 O.R. went on leave.	J.H.
"	28	6 a.m. 8.15 12.0 2.0 P 5.7 p.m. 6.0 P 11.30	Working Party 1 Officer & 50 O.R. No 2 section musketry lectures. Do. Working Party 1 Officer & 40 O.R. Battery travels from Hqrs. & Transport. interchanging and at LA CHAPELLETTE. do. & TEMPLEUX-LA-FOSSE by motor lorries. 10 O.R. 6 O.R. & 5 horses arrived from 13th Jock Horse Lines FRISE, 1 horse L.D. with septic poisoning & coming from sick. LIEUT. A.L. HERRIDGE & 2 O.R. returned from leave.	J.H.

Army Form C. 2118.

WAR DIARY
or
INTELLIGENCE SUMMARY.
(Erase heading not required.)

125 COMPANY,
MACHINE GUN CORPS.
APRIL 1917.

Place	Date 1917.	Hour	Summary of Events and Information	Remarks and references to Appendices
FRANCE Ref. Map 62 c 4 point	April 29	8.0 a.m. 10.15	Working Party. 1 Officer & 40. O.R. unloading coal at LA CHAPELLETTE.	
		12.0	2nd Lt. 2 & 3 returns with working party.	
PERONNE 1.27.F.		11.0	Transport inspection by S.O.C. Bde.	
		2.0 G	Gun Drill, cleaning guns, equipment, preparing for move.	
		4.0 p.m.	1 O.R. admitted to hospital sick off the strength.	
			LIEUT. N.G. SMITH proceeded on duty to Base Depot via R.E. Strength of Company at this date. 11 Officers & 190. O.R. (including 3 Officers & 60.O.R. attached, on leave etc.) & sick etc.) 8 riders & 41 L.D. horses (2 L.D. horses at AMIENS T/O sick)	
			1 L.D. horse shot by V.O. inflammation of the bowels.	
Ref. Map April 30 62 C N.E. 1 20.017 TINCOURT		a.m. 10.10	The Company moved by route march with transport to TINCOURT and billeted in empty house K.9.a.6.8. arriving at 12.50 a.m. Capt. R.V. GERY	
			1 LIEUT. R.W. LUCAS proceeded to 144 Bde. F.26.d.1.5 to reconnoitre front line. Coy HQrs. F.26.d.1.5	
			2 S.S. wagons were supplied by 15.44 Inf. Brigade return. 3 empty S.S. limbered wagons from stores were left at PERONNE & 5. O.R.	
			1.O.R. admitted to Field Ambulance, also 2/LIEUT. S. DICKINSON (influenza)	
			4. O.R. went on leave.	

Major Capt.
2. 5. 17.

Appendix 1.

The Company relieved the 143rd Machine Gun Company. The Transport under LIEUT. A.L. HERRIDGE remained at LONGAVESNES. Hqrs. Nos. 1 & 3 Sections & 1 gun of No. 4 section moved to SAULCOURT. (62c N.E. E.15.b.7.8.) No. 2 section & No 4 section less 1 gun relieved 2 sections of the 143rd Company at 8p.m. Relief completed by 10p.m. The front occupied by the 125th Bde stretches from 57c S.E. X.25.a.0.7 to 62c N.E. F.1.b.1.6 the left sector, from the latter point to 62c N.E. F.8.b.2.8. with the 8th Division on the left & the 48th on the right. No 2 Section was in the left sector with the 5th L.F. & No. 4 section with the 7th L.F. in the right sector. The guns occupied positions as shown on the attached map, infantry outposts being pushed out in front at night. The object of the positions occupied was to completely sweep the brigade frontage with a barrage of fire.

Spring Capt.
2.5.17

Appendix II.

Attached are reports forwarded during the month. The chief difficulty encountered was how to keep the Transport in good condition when working hard under bad weather conditions. Since the beginning of March when the horses were issued, 6 have died or been shot by order of the V.O., 4 from debility, 1 septic hoof & 1 enteritis. The Light Draught horses issued to the Company from Remount Depôt, though apparently sound, soon showed their weak points & did not appear to be sufficiently recovered for heavy work.

　　　　　　　　　　　　[signature] Capt.
　　　　　　　　　　　　2. 5. 17

R.G. 2.

Staff Captain,
 125. Brigade.

Sir,

Reference attached Report from my Transport Officer.

The forage issued to this Unit is in my opinion of such a poor quality that the horses are suffering from under-feeding and should not at present be put to the hard work expected of them.

I have had two horses die in the last fortnight from exhaustion, which is in my opinion entirely due to the poor quality of the oats and hay supplied (see sample herewith) and there are several animals in the Transport which need prolonged rest before they are fit to pull a fully loaded limber.

The Transport personnel is also very hardly worked, leaving billets between 6.a.m. and 7.a.m. and seldom returning until 5.p.m till 6.p.m. Little chance is given to them to get the harness cleaned, or to fit the newly issued and stiff Pack Saddlery.

I would represent that if it is in any way possible the Machine Gun Company Transport should be relieved of the stone and brick carrying duties allotted to them at present, at least one day out of three to rest the men and horses, to clean limbers, to get horses properly groomed, to clean harness and to fit the above mentioned Pack Saddlery.

I should like to place it on record that in my opinion and in the opinion of my Transport Officer, the transport of this Company from overwork, quality of forage above referred to and and the uses to which Machine Gun limbers are put to and horses removed from the strength of the Company, sick and died is not in any condition to stand a rapid move with full loads, and I would request that the Company may be granted some release from the work which is at present allotted to them.

4/4/17.

(signed) R.J. Gery. Captain.
O.C. 125th Machine Gun Company.

Ref:- A.L.H. 246.

In the Field
April 4th 1917.

From Transport Officer, 125th Coy. M.G. Corps.
To. Adjt. 125th Coy, M.G. Corps.

Sir,
    I beg to send you herewith a sample of the oats we have been receiving lately for your horses. As you will see for yourself they are of very inferior quality, with no body in them at all. The animals are deriving very little benefit from them as they seem to go right through without doing any good.

    In view of the fact that our horses are working every day I wish to respectfully point out that it is essential they should get substantial food given them.

    Believe me, Sir,
        Yours obedient Servant.
    (Signed) A. LESLIE HERRIDGE.
        T.O.

Ref. A.L.H. 250.

In the Field,
April 13th 1917

From Transport Officer, 125. Coy. M.G. Corps.
To. Adjt. 125 Coy. M.G. Corps.

Sir,

I beg to inform you that I have 13 horses requiring the attention of the veterinary officer. Particulars of ailments attached. The last visit of the veterinary officer was at Fuise and of the veterinary sergeant at Peronne on April 8th when I sent for him. I have to-day sent my sergeant down to Peronne requesting the immediate services of the veterinary officer. Some of our animals were issued from remount apparently fit but on getting into collar have broken down. The horses with sore chines have evidently suffered from the same complaint before. The horses suffering from debility have had the same feeding and have had no more work than the others.
I understand, Sir, that the A.D.V.S. has never inspected our animals since they were issued from remount.

Believe me, Sir,
Your obedient Servant.
(Signed) A. LESLIE HERRIDGE.
2/Lieut.

O.C. Transport Section,
125th Coy. M.G. Corps.

<u>Subject</u>   Tactical and Technical Lessons learnt during
             past month.
             ―――――――

Reference. B.M. 582.

A. <u>Tactical Lessons Learnt</u>:
(1). Absolute necessity for closer touch between Machine Guns, Lewis Guns & Infantry. Company Headquarters should be not less than 400 yds. from line held by guns, and in telephonic communication with Infantry Sub-Sector H.Q. The M.G. Coy Commander should be at these Advanced H.Q. and be backed up with his Sector Commanders (M.G.) by runners.
Orderly Room, Q.M. Stores, Transport and Reserve Section, if any, to be at Wagon Lines (say 3 miles behind the line) connected with Brigade H.Q by telephone.
See attached rough sketch.
Unless these advanced H.Q. are formed it is feared that it will be impossible for the M.G. Coy. Commander to control the guns adequately.

(2) <u>S.A.A.</u>
The advisability of incoming and outgoing Companies taking over and handing over a certain amount of both S.A.A. is brought to notice of Brigade. In the writers experience at least 60000 rounds per Company was treated in this way, thus freeing four limbers for any further transport purposes required.
The fighting limbers each carry 9,000 rounds, which it is submitted is sufficient for immediate and mobile purposes.
A certificate could be rendered to Brigade by M.G. Coy. immediately after each move, if necessary, as to the

                                                Cont

completeness of Bulk ~~Stores~~ S.A.A. handed and taken over.

(3). During the last operations too many guns were placed in the line. In the judgment of the writer four guns could have performed the duties allotted to seven, having a mobile reserve.
(see para 4.).

(4). Not enough use seems to be made of the undoubted use of Vickers Guns for Indirect Fire. Massed guns, not less than four, should be used from a rear position, either at the discretion of the Brigade Commander (sometimes detailed to M.G. Coy Commander) or as required by Section Commanders.
This could be done by guns in support and reserve.

B. Technical Lessons.

There is an urgent need for the re-issue of clinometers, field, to M.G. Coys. They were so issued at one time but were replaced by the elevating dial and spirit level, which as methods of putting correct elevation on guns, are very inaccurate.

21/4/17.

(signed) R.J. Gerry. Captain.
O.C. 125th Machine Gun Company.

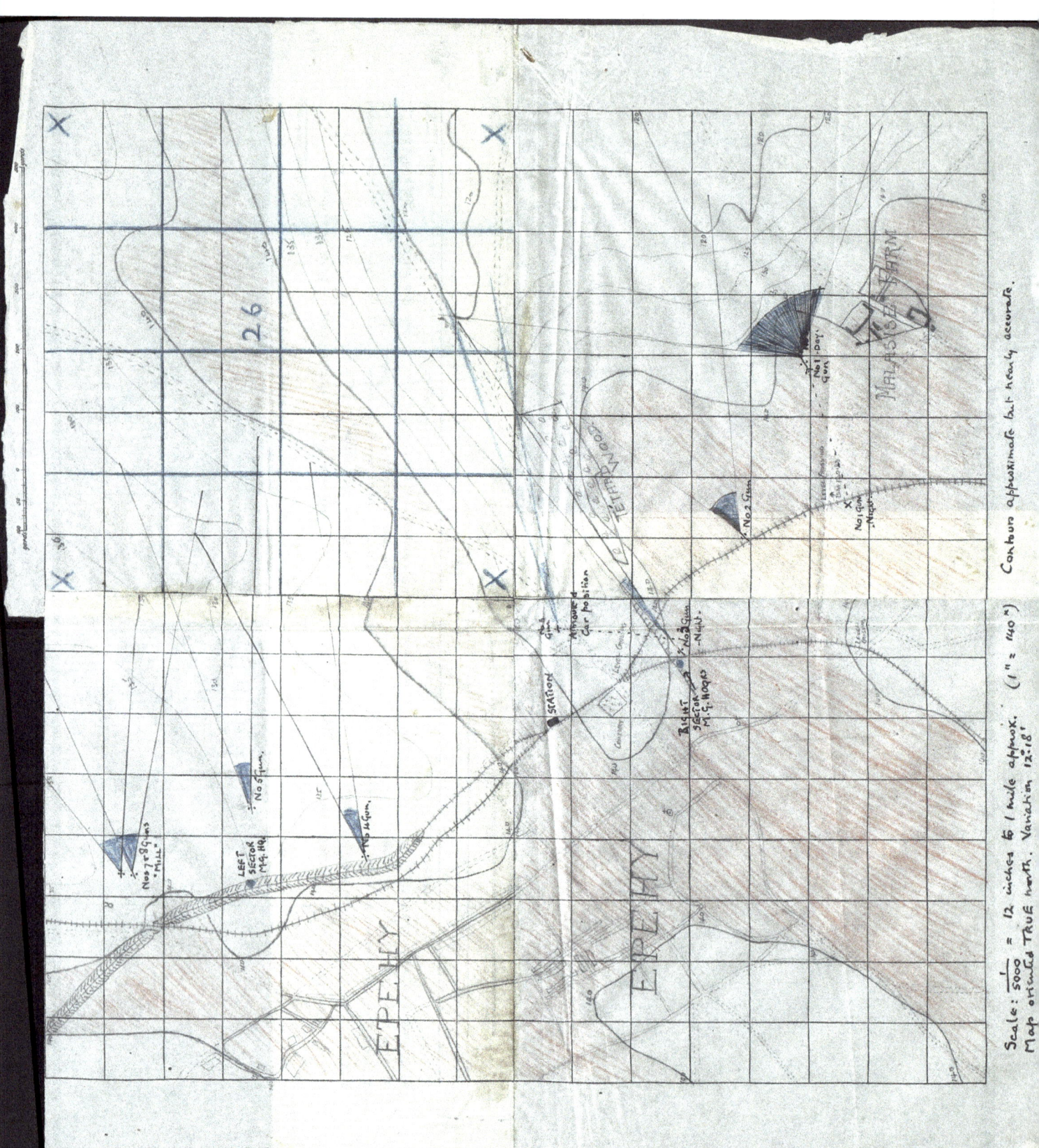

Scale: 1/5000 = 12 inches to 1 mile approx. (1" = 140") Contour approximate but nearly accurate.
Map oriented TRUE north. Variation 12.18°

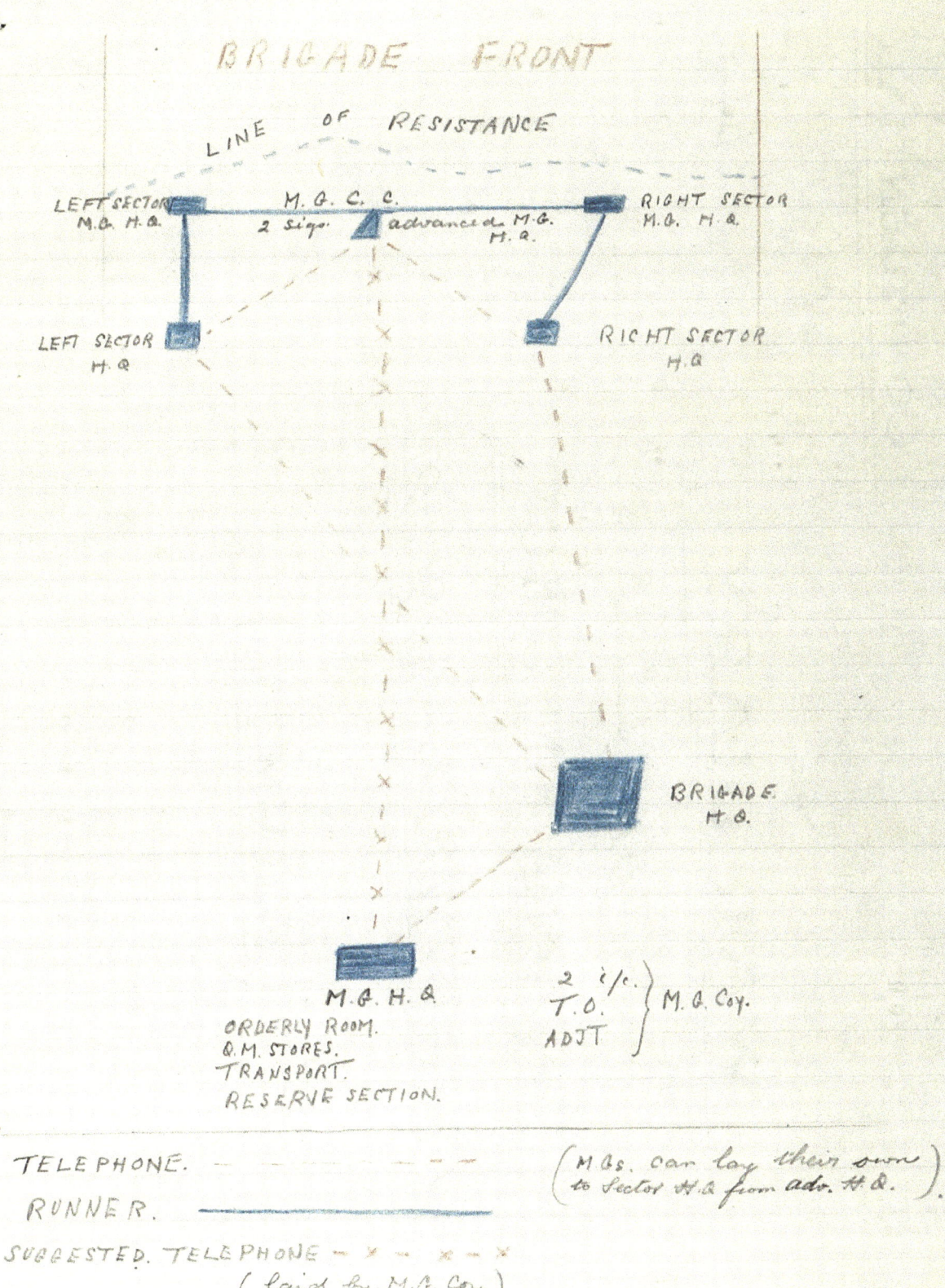

CONFIDENTIAL.

Vol 4

WAR DIARY.

OF

The 125th. MACHINE GUN Coy.

From May 1st, 1917 to May 31st., 1917.

(VOLUME V.)

Duplicate Copy.

WAR DIARY

Army Form C. 2118.

125TH MACHINE GUN COMPANY

INTELLIGENCE SUMMARY

MAY. 1917.

(Erase heading not required.)

Instructions regarding War Diaries and Intelligence Summaries are contained in F. S. Regs., Part II. and the Staff Manual respectively. Title pages will be prepared in manuscript.

Place	Date 1917	Hour	Summary of Events and Information	Remarks and references to Appendices
FRANCE TINCOURT. 28/Map. 20,000 Sheet 62cNE.Ed.3A. K.19.a.1.8.	May.1.	4.0 p.m.	4 Company moved by route march to VILLERS-FAUCON and relieved 2nd Lieut. T. Jaffe of 144 G.M.G. Coy. at 9.30 p.m. Left section joined Company from M.G.C. Base.	Appendix "A" 125 Bde. O.O. 11. of 30.4.617.
	May.2.	10.0 A.M.	4.0.R. proceeded on leave to U.K. C.Q.M.S. returned from leave to U.K. Remainder of Company moved by route march to VILLERS FAUCON and relieved H.Q. and Right Section of 144 M.G. Coy. in line. Coy. H.Q. at F.Kd.15. 2.0.R. proceeded on leave to U.K. Transport Brigade.	
	May.3.	11.30pm & 12.0 midnight	5.0.R. returned from leave to U.K. Associated advance of Brigade on right by barrage with 4 guns on line Copse A.25.a. - QUENNEMONT FARM inclusive. Fire from 11.30p.m. (zero) & 11.40p.m. intense and 4.40 h. am. to 12.0 midnight. Lewis Shoots were on line F.23.c.3.5- F.23.c.5.8. which was eleven by Haylig. B.	S&dD
	May.4.		4.0.R. proceeded on leave to U.K. 4.0.R. proceeded on leave to U.K.	
	May.5.	9.0pm	4 guns of left Sub. Section relieved by 4 guns 126 M.G. Coy. Relief section LRD Bates over night at DYNAMITE WOOD VILLERS-FAUCON. 2.0.R. proceeded on leave to U.K. T.O.R. proceeded on 4-8 Louis Special leave to BOULOGNE. 3.0.R. returned from leave to U.K.	Appendix "B" 125Bde.O.O. 12-3.5.1917.
	May.6.	9.0pm	Company Headquarters and remainder of Coy. relieved by 126M.G. Coy. Company billeted over night in DYNAMITE WOOD) VILLERS-FAUCON.	
	May.7.	10.0 am	Company moved by route march to LONGUESNES. E.25.6.3.3. Lieut. G. O'Kay and 2 other ranks proceeded to 4th Army Infantry School FLEXICOURT on a Course. 2.0.R. proceeded on leave to U.K.	
LONGUESNES E.25.6. 3.3	May 8.	9.0 pm	916.2 Section of 4 guns relieved Right Sub-Section 127M.G. Coy. in frontline. 2.0.R. proceeded on leave to U.K.	Appendix "C" 125 Bde.O.O. 14 - 6.5.1917.

Army Form C. 2118.

WAR DIARY

INTELLIGENCE SUMMARY

125TH MACHINE GUN COMPANY.

MAY 1917.

(Erase heading not required.)

Instructions regarding War Diaries and Intelligence Summaries are contained in F.S. Regs., Part II. and the Staff Manual respectively. Title pages will be prepared in manuscript.

Place	Date 1917.	Hour	Summary of Events and Information	Remarks and references to Appendices
FRANCE.				
LONGUENESSE E.25.6.3.3.	May 7.	7.0 p.m.	Company Headquarters and remainder of 127th M.G. Coy. relieved Company Headquarters and remainder of 127 M.G. Coy. in frontline at	
PEZ I ERE W.30.d.8.8.R.10.J	May 10.		W.30.a.8.8. (Sheet 57 S.E. 20000). 2.O.R. proceeded on leave to U.K. 2.O.R. 15th Lan. Fus. temporarily attached. 1.O.R. returned from Special Leave to BOULOGNE. 3.O.R. returned from leave to U.K. Situation normal.	
	May 11.		4 C.S.M. Perkins, C.H. left for U.K. to join officers Cadet Battalion, M.S.E. 1.O.R. to Field Ambulance. Situation normal.	
	May 12.		1.O.R. proceeded on leave to U.K. Situation normal.	
	May 13.		1.O.R. to Field Ambulance. 1 Officer (Capt. G.L. Wareham) and 1.O.R. returned from leave to U.K. Lieut. F.G. Smith 18th Lan. Fus. seconded M.G.C. struck off the strength 30.4.1917 on transfer to Special Brigade R.E. Authority 4 2nd Divisional Letter No. A. 357/440 dated 7/5/1917. 1 Lieut. A.E. Woolridge, attached from 16th Lan. Fus. seconded for duty with the Machine Gun Corps. Authority 4 2nd Divisional letter no. A. 357/440 dated 13/5/17. Situation normal.	
	May 14.		14.1.O.R. returned from leave to U.K. 1.O.R. admitted to hospital in England whilst on leave. Situation normal.	
	May 15.		1.O.R. from Field Ambulance. 1.O.R. to Field Ambulance. 1.O.R. to Hospital situation normal.	
	May 16.		1.O.R. to hospital. Situation normal.	
	May 17.		1.O.R. to hospital. Situation normal.	
	May 18.		Relieved by 3rd Cavalry M.G. Squadron at VILLERS FAUCON after relief 1.O.R. from leave to U.K. Billeted in DYNAMITE WOOD. 2.O.R. from duty left Coy. of signals.	Appendix "D" 125th M.G. CO. 16 - 16.5.1917

2353 Wt. W2541/1454 700,000 5/15 D. D. & L. A.D.S.S./Form/C. 2118.

WAR DIARY

125TH MACHINE GUN COMPANY

MAY 1917.

Army Form C. 2118.

(Erase heading not required.)

Place	Date 1917.	Hour	Summary of Events and Information	Remarks and references to Appendices
FRANCE DYNAMITE WOOD VILLERS FAUCON.	May 19.		1.O.R. from Field Ambulance. 1.O.R. to M.G. Course. Company Inspection.	Appendix "E" 23.6B.00/17
	May 20.		3.O.R. sick to Field Ambulance. Company moved by route march to EQUAN COURT, Camp V.II.a. (Sheet 57 SE 20000).	26.8.8./17 Appendix "F" 25B0.00/18
V.II.a.	May 21.		2.O.R. proceeded on leave to U.K. Advance party went into line with 6th M.G. Coy.	20/5/1.917.
	May 22.		1.O.R. from Transport Course ABBEVILLE Lieut R.E.F. Barrett proceeded on leave to U.K. 6th M.G. Coy. relieved by Bde. O.O. 18. Coy. H.Q. moved to DESSART WOOD. W.I.6.5.5. Lieut. H.B. Carlis & and 2.O.R. returned from M.G. Course, CAMIERS. 5.O.R. returned from leave Transport left at camp V.II.a.	
W.I.6.5.5.	May 23.		Transport Section moved to Coy. H.Q. DESSART WOOD. 3.O.R. returned from leave to U.K. 1.O.R. Temporarily attached to Brigade H.Q. as runner.	
	May 24.		1.O.R. reinforcement joined from M.G.C. Base Depot. 1.O.R. struck off strength as Instructor Divisional Anti-Gas School. 2.O.R. on leave to U.K. by	Appendix "G" 1758 de OO.19/24/5/17
	May 25.		5.O.R. returned from leave to U.K. Six right hand guns relieved	5th.15
	May 26.		124 M.G. Coy. moved to Brigade Transport lines NEUVILLE. Transport Section cleaned up and inspecting clothes. 1.O.R. to Field Ambulance.	8th.015 Appendix of relaxation 25B0.00
	May 27.		1½ Sections cleaned by Col. relieved by 177th M.G. Coy. 1½ sections Training 7.0 am. to 8.10.0 Remainder of Coy. 10.0am to 11.0am Sectional drill. 11.0am to 12.0 noon Staff rate 2.0 pm. squad drill. 3.0 pm to 4.0 pm Elementary drill.	19/24/5/17
YTRES. P.20.6.5.2.	May 28.		At 3.0 pm lecture on "French Warfare." 3.0 pm to 4.0 pm Remainder 9.0am-10.0am cleaning 2½ sections cleaning fighting aeroplane sights; 10.0 am – 12.30 pm Bathing and guns, three range shooting 2.0pm – 3.0 pm Lecture on "French Contact." 3 Coy. Cricket & change of clothing 2.0 pm. 4 O.R. returned from Leave 3.O.R to Hospital; 1.O.R to Fd. Amb. Sick; match. V2.O.R. on leave. 4.O.R. returned from leave by O.C., 1.10 pm & Corporals for cleaning limbers.	
	May 29.		10.0 am Inspection of Company by O.C., 1.10 pm & Corporals for cleaning limbers.	

Army Form C. 2118.

WAR DIARY

~~INTELLIGENCE~~ SUMMARY. 125TH MACHINE GUN COMPANY.

MAY 1917.

(Erase heading not required.)

Instructions regarding War Diaries and Intelligence Summaries are contained in F. S. Regs., Part II. and the Staff Manual respectively. Title pages will be prepared in manuscript.

Place	Date 1917.	Hour	Summary of Events and Information	Remarks and references to Appendices
FRANCE P.20.b.5.2.	May 29.	2.0 pm.	½ Coy parade at Transport lines for cleaning harness; 5.30pm Lecture by E.O.C. 125 Brigade to all officers and N.C.O's at H.Q. 1/6th Lanc. Fus. 1.O.R. to Field Ambulance.	
	May 30.	9.30 a.m.	Inspection of Company by O.C.	
		11.0 a.m.		
		11.30 p.m.	Sections at disposal of Section commanders.	
		2.0 pm.	Rough ground drill and attack.	
		4.0 pm.	1.O.R. to Field Ambulance. 2.O.R. on leave to U.K. 1.O.R. to hospital sick.	
	May 31.	10.0 a.m.	Inspection of Company by O.C.	
		2.0 p.m.	Inspection of Company, with Transport, by E.O.C. 125 Brigade.	
			2.O.R. on leave to U.K.	

Mur

Captain,

o.c. 125th Machine Gun Company.

Copy. Appendix "A"

Secret.

125th BRIGADE.   ORDER No. 11.

Ref. 62.C. 1/40,000.   30-4-17.

1. The 42nd Div. will relieve the 48th Div. in the Left Sector of III Corps. Command will pass to G.O.C. 42nd Div. at 10. a.m. May 3rd.

   42nd Div. H.Q. close at PERONNE, and re-open at K.11.a.7. 10.a.m May 3rd.

2. 125. Bde will relieve 144 Bde in Right Sector. Relief will be carried out in accordance with attached table, and is to be completed by night of 2/3 May.

3. Command of Artillery will pass to B.G.R.A. 42nd Div. at 10.a.m. May 2nd.

4. All details of relief to be made between Commanding Officers concerned.

5. Units going into line will leave caps and packs at Transport Lines. Only greatcoats and waterproof sheets will be taken up.

6. Commanding Officers will pay particular attention to continue all work on same lines as now being carried out. No cessation of work should occur.

7. Hour at which Command passes to 125th Bde. will be notified later.

8. ACKNOWLEDGE.

Issued at 5. a.m.   (signed) A.E. LAWRENCE.
                                                        Capt.
                                                        Bde Major.
                                                        125. Brigade.

Table to Accompany 125th Brigade Order. Number 11.

Unit.	Date.	From.	To.	Remarks.
1. 5th L.F.	April 30th	Nebocourt Farm	Camp K.S. Central not to arrive before 5.p.m.	C.O. and Coy. Commanders to report to 144 Bde. H.R. at 7.20 & 2.25 at 6.p.m. to reconnoitre line. 1 Officer per platoon & Coy at same time and remain in the line until Batt. arrives.
2. 5th L.F.	night 1/2 may.	K.S. Central	Right sub-sector of Right Bde. Front.	Time of relief by wire later.
3. 6th L.F.	may 1st	BUIRE.	Camp. S.E. of VILLERS-FAUCON not to arrive before 5.p.m.	Coy. Commander to report to 144 Bde H.Q. to reconnoitre line. 1 Off. per Coy. and 1 N.C.O. per platoon to report at same time and remain in line until Batt. arrives.
4. " "	night 2/3 may.	Camp S.E of VILLERS-FAUCON.	Left sub-sector of Right Bde Front.	Time of relief by wire later.
4th L.F.	may 1st.	CARTIGNY.	Camp K.S. Central not to arrive before 5. p.m.	
8th L.F.	may 2nd	DOINGT	Camp S.E of VILLERS-FAUCON not to arrive before 5. p.m.	
125. Bde. H.Q.	may 1st	PERONNE	TINCOURT.	Hour of start 10. a.m. H.Q close at 9. a.m. and re-open 11 a.m. TINCOURT.
125 T.M.B.	may 1st	PERONNE.	TINCOURT.	Hour of start 10-15 a.m. Billeting Party to meet Staff Capt. at TINCOURT CHURCH, 10. a.m.

—PTO—

(2)

Unit	Date	From	To	Remarks
125. Bde H.Q. 125. T.M.B.	May. 2nd	TINCOURT	F.20.b.2.5.	Hour of start 10. a.m.
125. M.G. Coy.	April 30.	PERONNE	TINCOURT	M.G. Coy. Commander and Off. i/c ½ Coy. in Left Sub-Sector to reconnoitre line after dusk
½ M.G. Coy.	night May 1/2.	TINCOURT	Left Sub-sector of Right Bde Front.	Off. i/c ½ M.G. Coy. in Right Sub-Sector to reconnoitre line after dusk
H.Q. M.G. Coy.	May 2nd	TINCOURT	M.G. Coy H.Q. in line.	
½ M.G. Coy.	night May 2/3.	TINCOURT	Right sub. sector of Right Bde Front.	

Copy.   Appendix "B".

SECRET

125th. Brigade Order. No. 12.

3rd May 1917.

1. 126th Bde. will relieve 125th. Bde as under :-

Unit.	Date.	Position in line.	Relieving Unit.
5th L.F.	Night 5/6.	Right Front Battn.	9th Manchesters.
8th L.F.	night 5/6.	Left Support Battn.	5th E. Lancs
6th L.F.	night 4/5.	Left Front Battn.	10th Manchesters.
7th L.F.	night 4/5.	Right Support Battn.	4th E. Lancs
½ 125th. M.G. Coy.	night 5/6.	Left sub-sector.	½ 126th M.G. Coy.
H.Q and ½ M.G. Coy.	night 6/7.	Right sub-sector.	H.Q and ½ 126th M.G.Coy.
125th T.M.B.	night 5/6.		
Bde H.Q.	night 5/6.		

2. All details of reliefs to be arranged between Commanding Officers concerned.

3. Relieving Units of 126th Bde will come under orders of G.O.C. 125th Bde. on entering Right Bde. area and relieved units of 125th Bde. will be under orders of G.O.C. 126th Bde until the 2 Commanders pass.

4. Completion of moves will be reported to both Bdes. giving map references.

5. ACKNOWLEDGE.

(signed) A.E. LAWRENCE. Capt
Bde. Major

SECRET   copy.   Appendix "C".

125th Brigade O.O. No. 14.   May 6th 1917

1. 125th Bde will relieve 127th Bde in Divisional Left Sector as per attached table. Commencing night 8/9th May. Relief to be completed night 9/10th May. All reliefs to commence not later than 9.30. p.m.

2. Completion of moves to be reported to 125th and 127th Brigades by Code word "JOCK."

3. All details of relief to be arranged between Commanding Officers concerned.

4. All area stores, maps and orders connected with Left Sector will be taken over. Units of 125 Bde will conform to the times of sending in reports etc. in vogue in 127th Bde until 125th Bde takes over. Particular attention is to be paid to continuing the same policy of work.

5. All units 125th Bde will come under orders of G.O.C. 127th Bde. on entering Left Brigade area until the Command passes.

6. All Coy Officers of support Battns will reconoitre the approaches to the GREEN LINE. Orders in case of attack will be the same as laid down by 127th Bde.

7. 127th Bde. will arrange the relief of 4 Companies holding BROWN LINE, composed of 2 Companies, 8th L.F. in railway cutting EPEHY., 1 Company 7th L.F. in LEMPIRE, 1 Company 7th L.F. in TOINE WOOD.

8. Brigade Transport lines will not be moved.

9. Units will report to the Staff Captain 24 hours in advance the number of wagons in excess of 1st Line required for move, giving time and place to report to.

10. ACKNOWLEDGE.

(signed) A.E. LAWRENCE.
Capt.
Brigade Major.
125. Brigade.

Issued at 8. p.m.

Table to accompany 125th Brigade O.O. No 14.

Unit	Date	From	To	Relieving	Remarks
1. 8th L.F.	night 8/9.	SAULCOURT	Left Front Battn.	6th Manchesters. H.Q. "THE WILLOWS" X 26c.	Relief of 2 Coys in BROWN LINE will be completed by 9 a.m. 10th. Coy and 1. M.G. gun Platoon will go into the line 24 hours in advance. Guides for this party at W.30.d.42 at 9. a.m. 9th.
2. 6th L.F.	night 8/9.	VILLERS-FAUCON.	Right Support Battn.	7th Manchesters H.Q. EPEHY. F.10.2.7.	
3. Part 125 M.G. Coy.	-do-	LONGAVESNES.	Right Front sector	Part 127th M.G. Coy. H.Q. PEIZIERE.	
4. ½ 125. Signal Section.	-do-	"	E.18c.	½ 127th Signal Section.	
5. 7th L.F.	night 9/10.	Camp. I.K.5. Central	Right Front Battn.	5th Manchesters H.Q. F.10.5.B.	Relief of 2 Coys in BROWN LINE will be completed by 24th. 1 Coy and 1 Off. gun Platoon will go into the line 24 hours in advance. Guides for this party to be arranged by C.Os. concerned.
6. 5th L.F.	-do-	VILLERS-FAUCON.	Left support Battn.	8th Manchesters H.Q. PEIZIERE. W.30.d.42.	
7. H.Q. and remainder 125 M.G.Coy.	-do-	LONGAVESNES.	Left sub-sector H.Q. in reserve	H.Q. & remainder 127 M.G. Coy.	
8. 125 T.M.B.	-do-	-do-	VILLERS-FAUCON	127 T.M.B.	
9. ½ 125 Signal Section and BDE H.Q.	-do-	-do-	E.18c.	½ 127 Signal Section and Bde Headquarters	

Copy.   Appendix "D"

SECRET

125th. Brigade O.O. No. 16.

Reference: 1/40,000. 62c.   16/5/17.
           1/20,000. 57c. S.E. and 62c. N.E.

1. The 42nd Division is being relieved by the 2nd Cavalry Division.

2. The 3rd Cavalry Brigade plus 1 Regiment will relieve 125th Brigade as per attached table.

   The 125th Brigade on relief will concentrate in reserve Brigade area and march to XV Corps area. Orders for this will be issued separately.

3. All details of relief will be arranged between C.Os. concerned. All units of 3rd Cavalry Brigade will come under the orders of G.O.C. 125th Brigade until command passes on completion of relief on night of 18/19. Completion of relief to be reported to 125th Brigade by code word "TEJE".

4. (a) All maps, papers, defence schemes, Intelligence summaries, and aeroplane photographs will be handed over on relief. A list of such papers will be issued later.

   (b) All orders re ammunition and trench stores will be issued later by Staff Captain.

   (c) Receipts for everything handed over will be obtained and sent to Bde. H.Q. at 10. a.m. 19th inst.

5. One Officer per Squadron and one N.C.O. per troop of A & B. Regiments will go into the line 24 hours in advance. 6th and 8th L.F. will supply them with all possible information with regard to our own and enemy's dispositions.

6. ACKNOWLEDGE.

                                        (Signed) A.E. LAWRENCE
                                                    Capt.
                                              Brigade Major.
                                                125. Brigade

Issued at:- 7.0 a.m.

Table to accompany 125th Brigade OO no.16.

DATE.	UNIT.	FROM.	TO.	RELIEVED BY.	REMARKS.
night 17/18	7th L.F.	Right Reserve EPEHY	Bivouac VILLERS-FAUCON	B. Regt. 3rd Cav. Brigade.	No movement on ST. EMILIE – EPEHY Road EAST. of E.12 & 7.0 before 9 p.m. Town major VILLERS-FAUCON will allot accommodation.
– do –	8th L.F.	Left Reserve PEIZIERE.	– do –	A. Regt. 3rd Cav. Brigade	– do –
– do –	125. M.G. Coy.		– do –	no. 3. M.G. Squadron.	1 man per gun in the line will remain for 24 hours with no.3.M.G. Squadron. Town major at VILLERS-FAUCON will allot accommodation.
– do –	125. T.M.B.	Line			TOWN MAJOR VILLERS-FAUCON allot accommodation.
18th	4th L.F.	VILLERS-FAUCON.	Reserve Bde Area SAULCOURT		Hour of start 9. a.m. Details to be arranged on 17th. To take over from B. E. LANCS.
– do –	5th L.F.	– do –	Reserve Bde Area. VILLERS-FAUCON.		– do –
night 18/19	6th L.F.	Right front	Bivouac. VILLERS-FAUCON.	B. Regt. 3rd Cav. Bde. and 1 Squadn. D Regt.	To take over from W. E. LANCS. Town major VILLERS-FAUCON will allot accommodation. 1 Squadn. D Regt. will relieve support Coy. 6th L.F.
– do –	B. Regt. 3rd Cav. Brigade.	Right Reserve.	Right front.	D. Regt. 3rd Cav. Bde.(less 1 Squad to Right support Coy.).	6th L.F. to supply guides at Right Reserve Batt. H.Q. for support Squad. at 9.30. A.m.
– do –	8th Lan Fus.	Left Front.	Bivouac. VILLERS-FAUCON.	A. Regt. 3rd Cav. Bde. and 1 Squadn. C. Regt.	Accommodation will be allotted by T.M. VILLERS-FAUCON. 1 Squadron. C. Regt. will relieve support. Coy. 8th L.F.

Continued (2).

DATE.	UNIT.	FROM.	TO.	RECEIVED BY.	REMARKS.
18/19.	A Regt. 3rd Cav. Bde.	Left Reserve.	Left Front.	C. Regt. 3rd Cav. Bde. (Wms. Squadron. to Left Support Squadron.)	8th L.F. to supply guides at Left Reserve Batn. H.Q. for Support Squadron at 9.30 p.m.
- do -	125.Bde.H.Q.	EPEHY	LONGAVESNES.	3rd Cav. Bde. H.Q.	
19.	125.M.G. Coy.	VILLERS-FAUCON.	- do -		Hour of start 9. am.
- do -	125.T.M.O.	- do -	- do -		- do -
- do -	6th L.F.	- do -	Reserve Bde Area. Camp K. 11 a.		Hour of start 9. a.m. To take over from 9th Manchesters
- do -	8th L.F.	- do -	Reserve Bde area. VILLERS-FAUCON.		Hour of start 9 a.m. To take over from 10th Manchesters

Administrative Instructions no. 3. issued in
Conjunction with Brigade O.O. no. 16.
———

1. RAILHEAD.   PERONNE.   May 19th (probable)
   Refilling point will be notified later.

2. All S.A.A. and grenades except those detailed in B.R.O. 76. dated 15th, will be handed over to incoming Units as French Stores.

3. All S.O.S. Signals, gold and silver rain Rockets, ground Flares, smoke cases and Very Lights will be handed over as French Stores.   Very Pistols will be retained by Units.

4. Orders with reference to the French Mortar Battery handing over Stokes Gun ammunition will be notified later.

5. The Machine Gun Coy will hand over all ammunition except that in belts, these will be brought from the line full.

6. Units will withdraw their establishment of tools but hand over any surplus to establishment.

7. Receipts will be obtained in duplicate for French stores. Receipts for ammunition and signals must give detail and map reference of all dumps handed over. One copy of receipt to be sent to Bde. H.Q. by 10. am on 19th inst.

8. Units 1st Line Transport may be moved from the Brigade Transport Lines any time after the 18th inst, to sites most convenient to Units.

9. Units will advise the 429 Coy. A.S.C. direct if they require their baggage wagons, giving time and place to report to.

10. All tents and shelters will be taken over by the Bde. to the new area. Transport arrangements will be notified later.

11. A dump for the Division is being formed in an Adrian Hut VILLERS-FAUCON. All stores, etc. surplus to what can be carried in baggage wagons and for which additional transport cannot be immediately provided, will be stored there. A guard for the dump will be provided, the following personnel being detailed by the Brigade :—
    1 Officer detailed by O.C. 5th L.F.
    1 Storeman from each unit.
   This personnel will be provided with 6 days rations

—cont—

Cont. 2.

from the 10th inst. These rations will be drawn & issued by Bde. H.Q.

12. The Bde. Dump at TINCOURT will be moved to VILLERS-FAUCON on the 17th inst. The following baggage wagons will be supplied by 429 Coy. A.S.C. and will report at TINCOURT Dump at 9. am on 17th inst.:-

    Each Battalion ..... 2. G.S. Wagons.
    M.G. Coy. ..... 1. G.S. Wagon
    T.M.B. ..... 1. G.S. Wagon
    Bde. H.Q. ..... 1. G.S. Wagon.

Units will send a loading party of 1 N.C.O + 8 men to be at TINCOURT at that time and an unloading party of same strength to be at VILLERS-FAUCON dump at 1 p.m that afternoon

13. Area Commandants detailed from Units of the Bde will be relieved at a date to be notified later by Officers of the Cav. Corps, and will proceed on relief to take over areas of the 20th Div as follows:-

		From	To
2nd Lieut A.S. Bergl	5th L.F.	No 2 area	NEUVILLE area
2nd " G. Schultz	5th L.F.	No. 3 area	YTRES.
2nd " H.B. Silverwood	6th L.F.	No 4 area	BUS-LECHOLLE

Area Commandants will take their Clerks and batmen with them.

14. Any honours and rewards for immediate recognition that have not been submitted in the interval will be forwarded to Bde. H.Q by 12 noon 18th inst.

15/5/17

(Signed) A.L. NEEDHAM. Capt.
Staff Capt. 125 Brigade

SECRET   Appendix "E"

COPY

125th BRIGADE O.O. No 17

1) 125th Brigade Group will march to-morrow as per attached table.

2) Distances of 400 yds will be kept between Battalions Field Coys etc. Units and their Transport will march closed up. L.G. limbers will march in rear of their respective Coys remainder of 1st line Transport in rear of their respective Units baggage wagons will march with the train.

3) Particular attention is to be paid to march discipline - calling to attention before halts - keeping to right of road - correct wearing of equipment - brakesmen only in rear of wagons.

4) Units will halt ten minutes before the clock hour and continue punctually at the hour. At each halt every man will take off his equipment (Rate of march 2½ miles an hour.)

5) Billeting parties consisting of an officer per unit and one n.c.o. per Company will rendezvous at LIERAMONT CHURCH at 9. a.m. and proceed in a formed body under the senior officer present and meet the Staff Captain at EQUANCOURT CHURCH at 10.30. a.m.. 3rd East Lancs Field Ambulance party will proceed to EQUANCOURT direct.

6) Completion of moves to be reported to Brigade Headquarters.

7) Watches to be synchronised by an officer with D.R.

8) Brigade Headquarters will close at LONGASVESNES at 1 P.M. and open at EQUANCOURT at 4 P.M.

9) ACKOWLEDGE by wire   (Signed) A.E. LAWRENCE

SECRET

ADDENDUM No 6 to 125st Brigade O.O. No. 16.

	FROM	TO
17th/18th	Right Battalion reserve JEPEHY.	K 11 A
	Left reserve PESIERES.	SAULCOURT
18th/19th	125 T.M.B.	Special camp in VILLERS FAUCON
	6 Lanc. Fus. Right Front.	VILLERS FAUCON
	8 " " Left "	VILLERS FAUCON
	125 M.G. Coy Line	Special camp VILLERS FAUCON
	Bde H.Q. Line	LONGAVESNES
	5 Lanc. Fus.	Bivouac VILLERS FAUCON } after striking
	7 " " SAULCOURT	Bivouac VILLERS FAUCON } camps
19th.	All Brigade K. 11 A	VILLERS FAUCON
20th	Strike camps and march to Divnl area.	

(signed) A. E. LAWRENCE
Captain
Brigade Major
125 Brigade

MARCH TABLE TO ACCOMPANY 125th BRIGADE OO NO 17

UNIT.	FROM.	TO.	ROUTE.	TIME.	STARTING POINT.	REMARKS.
Bde H.Q. and Personal Divn. Gas School.	LONGAVESNES	EQANCOURT	LIERAMONT-X roads 9.25.S - NURLU	1. P.M.	Road junctions E.19 c/9.51.5	
5 L.F.	SAULCOURT	Camp V.10.a	-do-	1.5.P.M.	X Roads E.14 @ 9.52.5.	Not to enter LIERAMONT before 1.27. P.M.
6 L.F.	VILLIERS FAUCON	-do-	-do-	1.14.P.M.	-do-	
7 L.F.	-do-	EQANCOURT	-do-	1.22.P.M.	-do-	
8 L.F.	-do-	-do-	-do-	1.31.P.M.	-do-	
M.G. Coy.	-do-	Camp VII.A	-do-	1.40 P.M.	-do-	
T.M.B.	-do-	-do-	-do-	1.42.P.M.	-do-	
n 29 Coy R.E.	-do-	FINS	Direct from NURLU	1.47 P.M.	-do-	
n 29 Coy A.S.C.	TINCOURT	Camp V.3.c				Not to enter LIERAMONT before 2.17 P.M. and to be clear of NURLU by 3.20. P.M.
3rd E. Lanc. Fld. Amb.	DOINGT	Camp V.11.b.	NURLU-FINS			Not to enter NURLU before 3.0. P.M.

SECRET   COPY   Appendix "F"

125 Brigade Warning Order No 18

1) 125th Brigade will relieve 60th Brigade in the line on night 22/23.

2) 125th Brigade will be disposed as follows:-

   Front Line.

   Right   8th L.F.
   Centre   5th L.F.
   Left   7th L.F.
   Reserve 6th L.F.

3) Commanding Officers of all 4 Battalions and M G Coy will report at 60th Brigade H.Q. W.1.b.17. at 2.P.M. to morrow to go round the line.

4) 1 Officer per Coy and one N.C.O. per platoon of each from line battalion will go into the line and remain there 24 hours in advance
   These parties will reach 60th Brigade H.Q at 7.P.M.

5) M G Coy will send one man per gun for front (4 guns) and intermediate (8 guns) lines with those parties at 7.P.M.

6) All details of reliefs are to be arranged between C.Os. concerned.

7) T.M.B. Will remain in present camp.

                                     A.E LAWRENCE
                                          Capt.,
20/5/17   Brigade Major
                                         125th Brigade

SECRET   Copy.   Appendix "G"

125. Brigade O.O. No. 19.   24-5-17.

1. The Front of the 42nd Division is being contracted and will be as shown on trace "A" after 6 a.m. June 1st.

2. On May 25/26. the 121st Brigade will take over from the Brigade present Southern Boundary (GREEN LINE.C) to Red line "A" on trace "B".

    8th L.F. will be relieved by 21st Middlesex Regt.
    5th L.F. by 13th Yorks Regt.

The 5th L.F. will go into Brigade Reserve with Headquarters and 2 Companies. GOUZEAUCOURT WOOD.
    1 Company   GOUZEAUCOURT WOOD at Q.22.C.3.2
    1 Company   INTERMEDIATE LINE. R.18.C.8.3-R.17.6.5.4.

This Company will take over accommodation vacated by the Company of Left Battalion at present garrisoning the INTERMEDIATE LINE, which will move up to R.13.a.3.7-R.13.a.5.0. and be in Battalion Reserve.

The Company of 5th L.F. in INTERMEDIATE LINE will not be used as Brigade Reserve until other troops have replaced it (see 125th Brigade Provisional Defence Scheme, para.6.)

3. The same night 6th L.F. will relieve 7th L.F. in the line

4. The 6 Guns 125th Machine Gun Company South of the Red Line "A"(trace "B") will be relieved by 121st Machine Gun Coy. on night May 25/26.

5. All details of relief to be arranged by C.Os. concerned. Completion of relief to be reported by code word "JOHN WILLY"

6. All maps (except 57 C.1/40000 and 1/10000) aeroplane photographs, Defence Schemes, tools, petrol tins, S.A.A. S.O.S. Signals, Grenades and Strombos horns will be handed over on relief and a receipt taken and sent to Brigade Headquarters. Mobile reserve of tools, S.A.A. and Battalion petrol tins will not be handed over.

7. On relief 7th and 8th L.F. and 1½ sections Machine Gun Company will go into billets at BERTINCOURT. Representatives to meet Staff Captain at Road Junction P.7.a.6.3. BERTINCOURT at 11.6 a.m. tomorrow

8. On completion of relief G.O.C. 121st Brigade will assume command of Sector South of Red Line "A". G.O.C. 125th Brigade retaining command from Red line "A" green line "D".

9. Orders for relief of 5th and 6th L.F. and Headquarters and remainder of Machine Gun Company by 178 Brigade

125th Brigade O.O. 19. (Continued).

on night 27/28 May later.

10. Acknowledge.

(Signed) A.E. Lawrence,
Captain)
Brigade Major,
125th Brigade.

SECRET   Appendix "H"

Addendum Number 1. To 125 Brigade a.o. Number 19

1) Remainder 125 Brigade will be relieved by the 177 Brigade on night 27/28 May.
   5 Leicesters relieve 6th L.F. in front line.
   5 Lincolns relieve 5 L.F. in reserve.

2) All details of relief to be arranged between Battalions and Machine Gun Company Commanders concerned.

3) Relief complete to be reported by code word "THUMBS.

4) 5th and 6th L.F. and Machine Gun Company will send guides tomorrow to Brigade Headquarters at 9.45 a.m. to conduct Commanding Officers.

5) All maps. (57c. 1/40,000 and 1/10,000) aeroplane photographs, Defence Schemes, tools, petrol tins, S.A.A. S.O.S. signals, grenades and Strombo's horns will be handed over and a receipt sent to Brigade Headquarters. Mobile reserve of S.A.A., grenades, tools, and petrol tins will not be handed over.

6) On relief Brigade Headquarters, 5th and 6th L.F. and 125th Machine Gun Company will be billeted in YTRES. Representatives to meet Staff Captain at TOWN-MAJOR'S office YTRES. 11.am. 27th inst.

7 ACKNOWLEDGE.

(signed) A.E. Lawrence
Captain
Brigade Major
125th Brigade

CONFIDENTIAL.

Vol 5

WAR DIARY.

— OF —

The 125th. MACHINE GUN COY.

from June 1st. 1917 to June 30th., 1917.

(VOLUME VI)

Army Form C. 2118.

WAR DIARY

INTELLIGENCE SUMMARY

125. MACHINE GUN COMPANY

JUNE 1917.

(Erase heading not required.)

Instructions regarding War Diaries and Intelligence Summaries are contained in F.S. Regs., Part II. and the Staff Manual respectively. Title pages will be prepared in manuscript.

Place	Date 1917 JUNE	Hour	Summary of Events and Information	Remarks and references to Appendices
FRANCE. YTRES. P.20.b.5.2. Sheet 57 SE NE 1/20,000	1.		3.O.R. to Field Ambulance.	MA45
	2.		4.O.R. joined Company from Machine Gun Corps Base Depot.	MA45
	3.	8.30 a.m.	Nos. 1 and 3 Sections moved by route march to H.Q. 125 M.G. Coy. HAVRINCOURT under Lieut. W.B. CARLISLE and Lieut. I. JAFFE to H.Q. 125 M.G. Coy. with barrage.	MA45
	4.	2.45 a.m. to 3.30 a.m.	avoir 126 M.G. Coy. with barrage. The following targets were engaged with 4 guns of No.1 Section under Captain G.S. WAREHAM at Q.9.a.7.4. and 4 guns of No. 2 Section under Lieut. W.B. CARLISLE at Q.3.c.6.2.:- K.34.b.4.2 to K.35.b.4.2 Rounds fired = 8100 Advance party of No. 1 Section went into line with 126 M.G. Coy. 1.O.R. returned from Field Ambulance.	Appendix "A" 125. Bde. O.O. 20 and attd. MA45
	5.		2.O.R. from Field Ambulance. 1.O.R. to Field Ambulance.	
	6.	9 p.m.	Relieved 126 M.G. Coy. in the line, taking over the following positions:- No.1 - Q.4.d.8.8; No.2 - Q.4.c.8.5; No.3 - Q.4.c.50.95; No.4 - Q.3.d.8.4; No.5 - Q.9 central No.6 - Q.9.c.2.7 (spare); No.7 - Q.3.c.7.4; No.8 - Q.9.b.8.4. Coy. H.Q. Q.13.d.8.8.	MA45
A.13.d.8.8.	7.		1.O.R. to hospital. I.O.R. from Field Ambulance. I.O.R. joined from Machine Gun Corps Base Depot.	
	8.		2nd Lieut. M.R.S. BREIDFORD occupying positions 4 guns of No. 4 Section under Lieut. M.R.S. BREIDFORD occupying positions at Q.9.b. to Q.9.d. for S.O.S. barrage on line N.34.c.4.6 & N.34.d.4.6 if required. The guns did not fire. The positions were occupied from dusk to dawn daily. 2.O.R. to Field Ambulance. 1.O.R. from hospital.	
	9.		Nos. 3 and 4 Sections under Lieut. M.R.S. BREIDFORD occupying positions on previous night. Two from Q.3.c.7.3 to Q.3.e. central for barrage work. Sections 126 M.G. Coy. attacked Q.5.c. from Cave to A.K.10.R. from Field Ambulance Lieut. R.E.F. BARNETT returned. Lieut. D.F. LARKINS at Q.5.c./2.8. fired 800 rounds One gun of No.1 Section under Lieut. H.B. One gun of No. 2 Section under Lieut. H.B. on Twood in K.34.c. during night 9/10 June.	

Army Form C. 2118.

WAR DIARY

INTELLIGENCE SUMMARY 125TH MACHINE GUN COMPANY.

JUNE 1917.

Place	Date 1917	Hour	Summary of Events and Information	Remarks and references to Appendices
FRANCE JUNE Q13.d.8.8. Sheets 57 SE] SW} NE3 }1/10000 NW4	9.	9/10 June night	CARLISLE at Q9c 75.10 fired 1250 rounds on N34c47 during night 9/10 June to prevent enemy snipers and trench mortars from carrying working parties on our front line. Infantry reported enemy bussier about than usual. Barrage guns also fired 1 phosy gun, 126 M.& Coy. in barrage line had 1 I.O.R. from Machine Gun Course at C.A.M.I.E.R.S. 2. C.R. from same I.O.R. from Field Ambulance. I.O.R. wounded in action. I.O.R.& invalided. 2 to School on Course.	
	10.	night	One gun of No.1 Section under Lieut. D.F.LARKINS engaged target as on previous night. 100 rounds were fired. One gun of No.2 Section under Lieut. H.B.CARLISLE engaged target as on previous night. 1250 rounds were fired. Infantry report favourable as on previous night. Two guns of No.3 Section under Lieut. M.A.S.BREEDFORD at Q9a1.8 fired 700 rounds during night on road in HAVRINCOURT from N27d4.78 N27d.7.3. One gun of No.3 Section under Lieut. R.E.F.BARNETT at Q10c 9.7. fired 850 rounds on N34c 4.7 in bursts during night. 12 guns on barrage lines at usual, i.e. 8 guns 126 M.& coy and 4 guns of Offc. Coy 246 M.G.	
	11.	night 11/12.	1 I.O.R. to hospital. 1.O.R. for dental treatment. One gun of No.1 Section under Lieut. D.F.LARKINS at Q5c.2.8 fired 700 rounds on N28c during night. One gun of No.2 Section under Lieut. H.B.CARLISLE at Q9c 75.10 fired 1250 rounds on N34d1.2 during night. One gun of No.3 Section under Lieut. M.A.S.BREDFORD. at Q9a1.8 fired 1500 rounds on road in HAVRINCOURT N27d4.78 N27d.7.3 during night. One gun of No.3 Section under Lieut. R.E.F.BARNETT at Q10c 9.7 fired 100 rounds on N34 c 4.7 during night. Barrage guns as for previous night. Q15 a 6.5. into INTERMEDIATE LINE. One gun at Q9 c. central moved to Q8 c. 9.6. into INTERMEDIATE LINE. One gun at Q3 c. 7.4 moved to Q15 a.2.8 into INTERMEDIATE LINE. One gun at Q9 c 2.7 moved to Q10 c 9.7. fired 100 rounds much 13.	

Army Form C. 2118.

WAR DIARY

INTELLIGENCE SUMMARY 125TH MACHINE GUN COMPANY

(Erase heading not required.)

JUNE 1917.

Place	Date	Hour	Summary of Events and Information	Remarks and references to Appendices
FRANCE Q13.d.8.8.	JUNE 1917 12.		Lieut H.B.CARLISLE proceeded on leave to U.K. 2nd Lieut. S.DICKINSON rejoined from sick leave to U.K. 2nd Lieut. S. DICKINSON recorded for service with the Machine Gun Corps 9.2.1917. Barrage positions occupied during night. N.C.O's & 15 P.O.R's joined from Machine Gun Corps Base Depot. 2 O.R. from Head to U.K.	
	13.	Night 13/14.	The following operations were carried out by supporting line 9a.1.5 & 9c.6.8.5.— "A" barrage 1.32 a.m. to 1.36 a.m. 3 guns under Captain R.U.GERY fired on line K34d.6.36. K34d.4.4. 3 guns under Lieut. M.A.S.BREIDFORD and 2nd Lieut. T.JAFFE fired on line K13 c.4.0 & K34.c.1.7. Six guns mentioned above fired on line K34.c.7.5 to K34.c.5.5.	
	14.		"B" barrage 1.36 a.m. to 1.39 p.m. K34.c.7.5 to K34.c.5.5. "C" barrage 1.46 a.m. to 1.50 a.m. 3 guns under Captain R.U.GERY fired on line K34.c.7.7 to up TRESCAULT HILL VALLEY. 5,250 rounds were fired. Barrage of 8 guns 126 M.G. Coy. assisted. 2 O.R. reinforcements joined from Machine Gun Corps Base Depot. 2 guns of No.3 Section under 2nd Lieut. S. DICKINSON relieved 2 guns of 27 M.G. Coy. on left of our front line. Barrage on wood.	
		Night 14/15.	Two guns of No.3 Section under Lieut. M.A.S.BREIDFORD fired on wood in K33.b.a.d on K34.a.1.7. 2000 rounds were fired. 150 rounds on the gun of No.1 Section under Lieut. D.F.LARKINS fired forty degrees. M.G.15 enemy working party at K34.c.8.0 at 12.15 P.M. 1917. Lieut. G.C.N.DAY and 2 O.R. rejoined from course at 4th Army Infantry School 3 O.R. proceeded to Divisional Signal & School on course. 3 O.R. returned from leave to U.K.1 O.R. to Field Ambulance. 1 O.R. wounded in action.	
	15.	Night 15/16.	Two guns of No.1 Section at 9 a.1.8. under Lieut. M.A.S.BREIDFORD fired 3000 rounds on N.34.d 6.38 & K34.d.1.8. One gun of No.1 Section under Lieut. D.F.LARKINS fired 250 rounds on K29.c.2.7 during day. 15th June. 1 O.R. rejoined from Divisional Anti-Gas Course.	
	16.			

Army Form C. 2118.

WAR DIARY
INTELLIGENCE SUMMARY. 125TH MACHINE GUN COMPANY.

JUNE 1917

(Erase heading not required.)

Instructions regarding War Diaries and Intelligence Summaries are contained in F.S. Regs., Part II. and the Staff Manual respectively. Title pages will be prepared in manuscript.

Place	Date 1917 JUNE	Hour	Summary of Events and Information	Remarks and references to Appendices
FRANCE Q13d5.8.	16.	6.30pm	One gun of No. 4 Section under Lieut. D.F.LARKINS fired 120 rounds on enemy parties in N28 C.5.7. and at 6.4.5pm on N28 C.6.7.	
	night 16/17.		Six guns of Nos. 1 and 3 Sections under Lieut. M.A.S.BREIDFJORD engaged the following targets :- N33 B.20.55 (neutralized enemy machine gun); H.B.3 65.8 ; H 33 B.65.90 ; N 33 C.40.6. 6 t N 3 C.all 8.8000 rounds just neutralized	see A19
	17.		2.O.R. rejoined from duty at 111 Corps school. One gun of No.4 Section under Lieut. D.F.LARKINS fired 100 rounds on N28 C.8.7. and N2.8.C.8.6. during day.	
	night 17/18.		Two guns of No.1 Section under 2nd Lieut. S. DICKINSON fired 2000 rounds on N34 C. central and wood in N33 B. Enemy machine gun in wood N33 b neutralized after worrying our working party on a new emplacement.	
	18.		1.O.R. from Field Ambulance. No. 8666. C.S.M. SWEET J.J. joined from 196th Machine Gun Company as Company Sergeant Major.	
	night 18/19.		Six guns of Nos. 1 and 3 Sections under Lieut. M.A.S.BREIDFJORD engaged the following targets during night from line Q9a.1.8 t Q8. 665.8.85 :- N 27 d 80.05 ; N 38 d a 15.50 ; N 33 d a 12.9 ; N 33 65.8 ; N 33 63.95 ; N 33 B.25.65. 6000 rounds were fired.	
	19.		One gun of No. 4 Section under Lieut. D.F.LARKINS fired 200 rounds on N28 C. Barrage guns no longer required. Section in INTERMEDIATE LINE relieved by Section of 126 M.G. Coy. under Lieut. GREEN-KELLY.	
	night 19/20.		Two guns of No.1 Section under Lieut. M.A.S.BREIDFJORD engaged the following targets during night from line Q 9 a 1.8 t Q 9 a 0.5.85 . i.e. SHROPSHIRE SPUR N 3 C. central t N 3 4 a 6.0. 1500 rounds were fired.	
	20.		1.O.R. proceeded on leave to U.K. 1.O.R. to Field Ambulance. 1.O.R. from Case to U.K. 2.O.R. from Field Ambulance. 2.O.R. transferred to the Machine Gun Corps M.G. from 1/5th Lan. Fus. (T.F.) and posted to this Company from 19/6/17.	

5.

Army Form C. 2118.

WAR DIARY

INTELLIGENCE SUMMARY. 125TH. MACHINE GUN. COMPANY.

(Erase heading not required.)

JUNE 1917.

Instructions regarding War Diaries and Intelligence Summaries are contained in F. S. Regs., Part II. and the Staff Manual respectively. Title pages will be prepared in manuscript.

Place	Date 1917 JUNE	Hour	Summary of Events and Information	Remarks and references to Appendices
FRANCE Q34B58	20.		Re-organization of guns in front line completed. Guns were then in the following positions:- No.1 – Q4d1.6; No.2 – Q4c 95.65; No.3 – Q3d65.75; No.4 – Q3d 5.5.80; No.5 – Q3c 45.70; No.6 – Q26 85.50; No.7 – Q2e 40.75 (daylight firing).	
			1 O.R. to Field Ambulance. 3 O.R. from Field Ambulance. 1 O.R. from hospital.	
	21.		2 O.R. to Field Ambulance. 3 O.R. from Field Ambulance. 1 O.R. from hospital.	
			1 O.R. on leave to U.K.	
	22.		1 O.R. from leave to U.K.	
YPRES P.20.C.3.7	22/23	Night	Relieved by 126th Machine Gun Company in the line. Company moved by route march to YPRES. Headquarters and No.4 Section moved to YPRES Lunatic Asylum P20 C 5.2. One Section (No.2) relieved one section 126th Machine Gun Company in the INTERMEDIATE LINE taking over the following positions:- No.26 – Q15 a 6.5.1; No.27 – Q15 a 2.8; No.28 – I18 e 9.8; No.29 – I7 b 8.4. Two Sections, under 2nd Lieut. R.L. HERRIDGE and 2nd Lieut. S. DICKINSON respectively relieved two sections 126th M.G. Company in the SECOND LINE, taking old the following positions:- No.1 – Q136.6.3; No.2 – P15d 9.7; No.3 – A18 a 7.9; No.4 – P12 c 0.5 80; No.5 – P5d 8.5; No.6 – P5d 8.5; No.7 – P5d 8.7.0; No.8 – J36 c 0.1. Also three battle emplacements an embankment near J36 c 0.1 what can be occupied by No.4 5, 6 and 7 guns if line is captured and attacked.	as appendix "B".
	23.		1 O.R. on leave to U.K.	
	24.		2nd Preliminary orders for rapid move attached	
	25.		1 O.R. to hospital. 1 O.R. from duty at III Corps Signalling School.	
	26.	3 p.m.	No.4 Section relieving No.3 Section in Right Section, 2nd Line; No 3 returning to C.H.Q. at YPRES.	
	27		Lieut. M.R.S. BREDFORD & 3 O.R. proceeded to Machine Gun School CAMIERS, France.	
	28		Nil	
	29		1 O.R. on leave to U.K.	

Army Form C. 2118.

WAR DIARY
or
INTELLIGENCE SUMMARY.
(Erase heading not required.)

125th Machine Gun Company

June 1917.

Place	Date 1917	Hour	Summary of Events and Information	Remarks and references to Appendices
YPRES. P.20.c.3.7	June 30	3p.m	No 3 Section relieved No 2 Section in Intermediate Line : No 2 Section returning to C.K.9 at YPRES. I.O.R. on leave to U.K. 2 off. attached showing Brigade Front Line in the Line Coy of Tactical & Technical Zones during month appended.	Appendix C. Appendix D.

Muir
Captain
Commanding 125th Machine Gun Company

30. 6. 17

Appendix "B"

M.L.
PRELIMINARY INSTRUCTIONS.

Ref. 1/40,000 MAP Sheet
57c.
                                                                   June 24th 1917.

1. The Brigade is now in Divisional Reserve.

2. The Company (less three Sections) will be prepared to move at 30 minutes notice on receipt of order "Stand To". On receipt of order "Stand To" guns complete, with requisite bulk and belt S.A.A. will be dumped on parade ground, and will be loaded on limbers immediately on their arrival.

3. The Company may move to one of four rendez-vous as under:-
   (a) Cross roads R.23.a.0.4. (NEUVILLE via YTRES and GENERATING STATION). Order of March RF, (less two Companies), CB, ML. (less three Sections) AE.

   (b)   -do-

   (c) Cross roads R.10.c.4.7. (RUYALCOURT via R.9.d.central). Order of March AE, RF. (less two Companies), CB., ML. (less three Sections).

   (d) Cross roads R.1.c.9.2. (NORTH of BERTINCOURT). Order of March as in (c).

4. Company (less three Sections) will parade on receipt of order "Stand To" on Alarm Post facing W.W. Dress:- Full Marching Order with Packs (all ranks).
The Company will parade as strong as possible, less the C.Q.M. Sgt. and ... fatigue of three men to be detailed in advance by the C.Q.M. Blankets will be left and collected by C.Q.M.Sgt. immediately. Rolled as usual and dumped together with any stores left behind. Officers' Valices will be packed at once and dumped. All Officers' Servants and Mess Corporal will move with the Company.

5. Rations.
On receipt of order "Stand To" each man will be issued with one day's preserved rations.
Water bottles will be kept filled.

6. Packs.
Packs will always be packed as laid down.

7. Sleeping.
Men may remove their clothes but will sleep so as to be ready to fall in complete in 15 minutes.

8. Iron Ration.
Attention is called to correct manner of carrying Iron Ration as laid down herewith.

9. Stand To.
On receipt of order "Stand To" the guard will immediately rouse the Camp without further instructions. The Company will fall in quietly and without noise.

10. Signallers.
Signallers will carry flags and telephones with two miles of wire. N.C.O. in charge will detail one man to remain behind in charge of remainder of stores.

Pte. Benton will remain with Orderly Room Stores, supervise their packing and proceed with R.S. Limber.

11. **Water Cart.**
Water Cart will be filled each night by 9-0 p.m. and remain filled during night.

(Signed) R.V.GENY. Captain.

O.C. M.L.

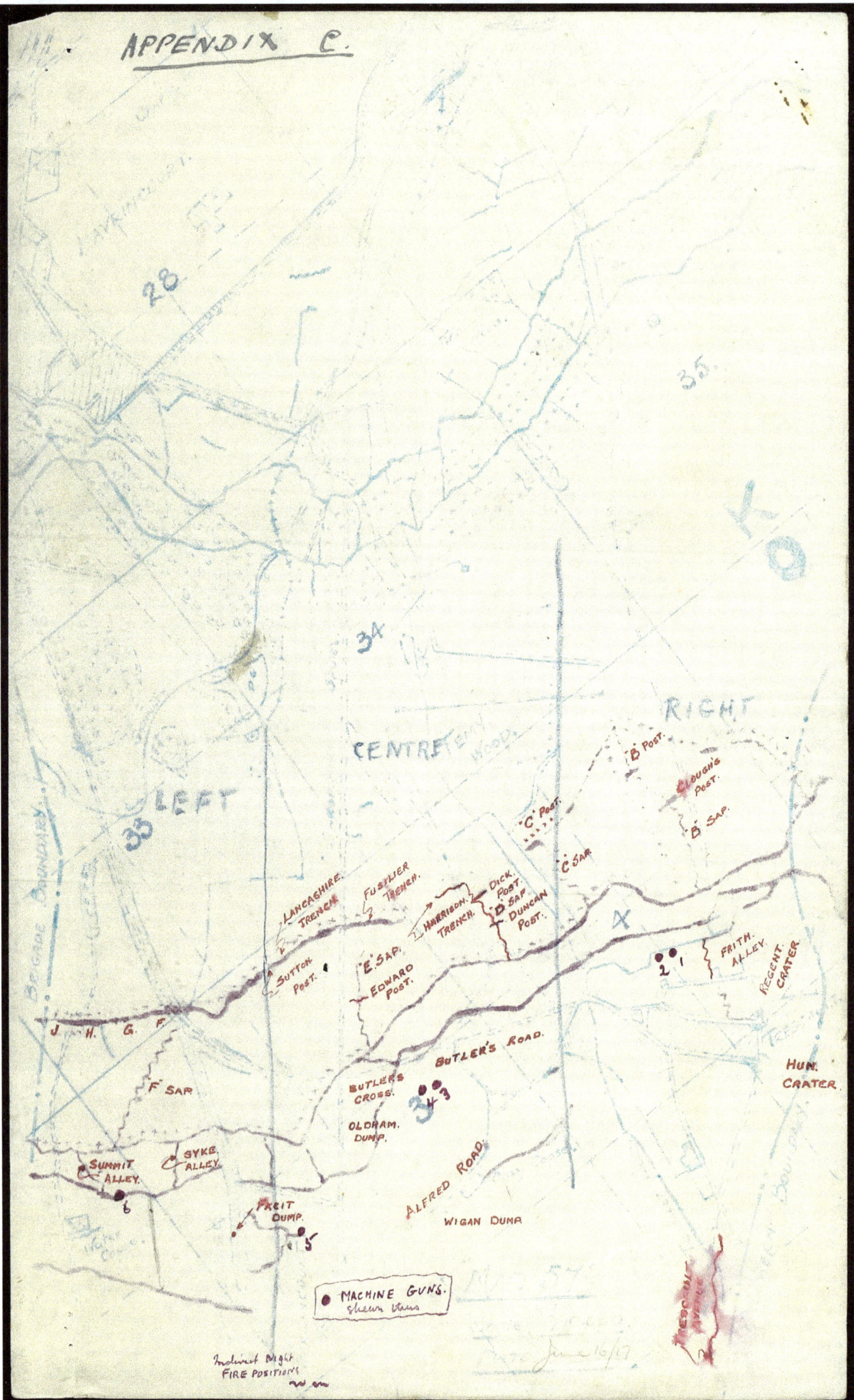

Appendix D.

R.G.160.

M. L.

TACTICAL AND TECHNICAL LESSONS LEARNT DURING JUNE 1917.

###############

(1) <u>TACTICAL</u>.

    1. General utility of Vickers guns in annoying enemy during "crystallisation period" after an advance.

    2. Importance of night firing, and its continuous use.

    3. Utility of acustoming Infantry to havings M.Gs fired over their heads.

    4. Importance of giving enemy twice as much as he gives you.

    5. Generally, the good effect of firing from Machine Guns, from in rear has on the Infantry in front.

6. <u>DEFENSIVE SCHEMES</u>. Great difficulty in adequately controlling Ravines, valleys etc. The sides may be swept by M.G.Fire (Usually obliquely) but it appears that Lewis Guns should be used for controlling the bottom of such valleys. Would it be possible for a small number of Lewis guns to be attached to the Machine Gun Company for defensive purposes only. These could then be co-ordinated in the M.G. defence of the particular sector, come under the control of the M.G. Officer in charge (Under the orders of the O.C. Sector), and be rationed and supplied by the Company.

7. <u>BARRAGE FIRE</u>. No actual experience of barrage fire has been obtained, but guns have been laid nightly for overhead indirect fire. Certain technical difficulties have occurred which are dealt with below.

(2) <u>TECHNICAL LESSONS LEARNT</u>.

1. <u>AIMING MARKS</u>. Luminous paint should be issued for these for night firing, also for "U" of Tangent Sight and blade of fore-sight. Alternatively the old siege lamp might be re-issued and a larger night firing box used

2. <u>SCREENS - FLASH</u>. Experience goes to show that the best form of screen is the ordinary blanket, canvas or hessian skein barrier, blanket being the best.

This form cannot however be used in daylight if it is necessary to conceal the flash, and when firing from in front of woods etc. the modified form constructed of a cylinder of rabbit wire and material can then be used.

3. CLINOMETERS.   These combined with an angle of sight instrument would be an advantage, as the level and dial is not accurate.

4. TELESCOPIC SIGHTS.   If a good telescopic sight was issued, it would be possible to do muchn useful sniping work and wowry the enemy.

War Diary
of
125 Machine Gun. Coy.
For
July 1917.
Vol VII.

Army Form C. 2118.

WAR DIARY
or
INTELLIGENCE SUMMARY
(Erase heading not required.)

125TH Machine Gun Company

Place	Date	Hour	Summary of Events and Information	Remarks and references to Appendices
FRANCE Map.Ref. Sheet 57d P.20 G.3,7. 1/40,000	July 1st		1 O.R. on Leave.	initld
	2nd		1 O.R. to Field Ambulance. 1 O.R. on Leave. 1 Officer (Lieut. A. Clymer 1/8th Lan.Fus.) attached	initld
	3rd		1 O.R. to Field Ambulance.	initld
			to Company as Transport Officer.	
	4th		1 O.R. to Hospital. Lewis Gun m.g.s. allowed not set up in interruption or complete by in personnel	initld
	5th		1 O.R. on Leave. (Cadet Battn.) 1 O.R. taken on strength from Divisional Gas	initld
	6th		1 O.R. to U.K. (Cadet Battn.) 1 O.R. on Leave. 1/40,000 A.29. a 5.1. for training	initld
A.29. a.5.1.	7th		Moved from to Map.Ref. 57c 1/40,000 A.29. a 5.1. for training	initld
			School. 1 O.R. on Leave.	initld
	8th		1 O.R. on Leave.	initld
A.29 b	9th		Moved Camp. 1 O.R. re-joined from Leave.	initld
7.5.	10th		1 O.R. on Leave. 1 O.R. (Attached) transferred to M.G.C. from 1/7th Lan.Fus. (L/Cpl. Gill)	initld
	11th		1 Officer (2nd.Lieut I. Jaffe) and 2 O.R. to 4th Army School of Signalling.	initld
	12th		1 O.R. (C.M.M.S.) to U.K. (Cadet Battn.)	initld
	13th		1 O.R. to Field Amb. 1 O.R. re-joined from Leave.	initld
	14th		2 O.R. to Field Amb.	initld
	15th		5 O.R. on Leave. 2 O.R. from Field Amb.	initld
	16th		1 O.R. to Field Amb. 1 O.R. re-joined from Leave.	initld
	17th		1 O.R. to Hospital.	initld
	18th		2 O.R. re-join from Leave.	initld
	19th			
	20th		1 O.R. to Field Amb. 2 O.R. re-join from Leave.	initld
	21st		5 O.R. on Leave to U.K.	initld
	22nd		1 O.R. re-joins from Leave.	initld
	23rd		1 O.R. to Field Amb. 1 Officer (Lieut. R.W.Lucas-Lucas) re-joins Company from 1/6th Lan.Fus. attached	initld
	24th		1 O.R. re-joins from Leave. Company Inspected by the G.O.C. 2 P.M.	initld
	25th		1 O.R. to Field Amb. 1 O.R. re-joins from Field Amb.	initld
	26th		2 O.R. on Leave.	initld
	27th		1 Officer (Lieut. R.W.Lucas-Lucas) admitted to Field Amb. 1 Officer and 2 O.R. re-join from M.G.School, CAMIERS.	initld
	28th		1 O.R. to Field Amb. 6 O.R. on Leave.	initld
	29th		1 O.R. to Machine Gun School, CAMIERS.	initld
	30th		1 O.R. to Hospital. 1 O.R. re-joins from Leave.	initld
	31st		4 O.R. re-join from Leave. 9th to 31st Company and Section Training.	initld

Wyly Captain.
o. 125 M.G. Coy.

CONFIDENTIAL.

WAR DIARY
- for -
125TH MACHINE GUN COMPANY.
- from -
AUGUST 1ST.1917 to AUGUST 31ST.1917.

(VOLUME VIII.)

Army Form C. 2118

WAR DIARY or INTELLIGENCE SUMMARY

125TH MACHINE GUN COMPANY.
AUGUST 1917.

(Erase heading not required.)

Instructions regarding War Diaries and Intelligence Summaries are contained in F.S. Regs., Part II. and the Staff Manual respectively. Title Pages will be prepared in manuscript.

Place	Date August	Hour	Summary of Events and Information	Remarks and references to Appendices
Map.Ref. Sheet 57c. 1/40,000 A.29.b.7.5.	1.		Holiday "MINDEN DAY"	JMc.
	2.		Company Training. Emplacements and Night Operations.	JMc.
	3.		Company Training. Route March.	JMc.
	4.		Company Training. Range Firing.	JMc.
	5.		Sunday.	JMc.
	6.		Company Training. Combined Drill, Barrage Drill, Entrenchments.	JMc.
	7.		Section Training. Tactical Scheme.	JMc.
	8.	8-15 to 5-30	Section Training. Barrage Drill, Fire Direction, Gas Drill.	JMc.
	9.		Scheme LOUPART WOOD, occupying defensive positions.	JMc.
	10.	8-30 to 12-30	Route March, COURCELLES LE COMPTE – ABLAINZEVILLE – LOGEAST WOOD FORREST – X Roads G.9.b CONTECOURT. 11 miles.	JMc.
	11.	2-0 to 4-0 pm.	Barrage Drill.	JMc.
	11.	6-30 to 7-0	Gas Drill.	JMc.
		8-30 to 12-15	Physical Training, Barrage Drill, Lecture, Use of Clinometer and Compass, Practical Fire Direction.	JMc.
	12.		Church Parade.	JMc.
	13.	8-45 to 5-30	Scheme LOUPART WOOD, Laying out Barrage lines of fire	JMc.
	14.		ditto Barrage Fire with Ball Ammunition.	JMc.
	15.	8-30 to 12-30	Overhauling Guns Etc. Barrage Drill, Inspection of guns by C.O.	JMc.
	16.	8-30 to 12-15	Physical Training. Lecture by Section Officers, Barrage Drill, Experiments carrying guns and equipment in action.	JMc.
		2-0 to 4-0	Care and cleaning, Points before, during and after firing etc.	JMc.

1875 Wt. W593/826 1,000,000 4/15 J.B.C. & A. A.D.S.S./Forms/C. 2118.

Army Form C. 2118

WAR DIARY
or
INTELLIGENCE SUMMARY
(Erase heading not required.)

125TH MACHINE GUN COMPANY.
AUGUST 1917.

Instructions regarding War Diaries and Intelligence Summaries are contained in F. S. Regs., Part II. and the Staff Manual respectively. Title Pages will be prepared in manuscript.

Place	Date AUGUST	Hour	Summary of Events and Information	Remarks and references to Appendices
FRANCE Map.Ref. Sheet 57c. 1/40,000 A.29.b.7.5	17.	8-30 to 12-30	Digging Trench Slits for Barrage for Brigade Scheme.	M/c
	18	2-0 a.m. to 8-0 a.m.	Brigade Scheme attack supported by Barrage Fire.	M/c
	19		Church Parade.	M/c
	20	8 a.m. 9 a.m.	Camp Struck. The Company moved by route march to BOUZINCOURT via ACHIET LE PETIT - MIRAUMONT - BEAUCOURT - MESNIL - MARTINSART. Occupied Camp at Point ½ mile S.E. of BOUZINCOURT on ALBERT Road.	M/c
Lens 11. 1/1000,000 H.6.	21.	9-15 to 12-15	Physical Training, Repacking Liners and checking Stores.	M/c
	22.	5 a.m. 9-11 8 p.m.	Company parade for entrainment at ALBERT Left ALBERT. Detrained at GODEWAERSVELDE. Marched to Camp at L.15.d.5.4. via ABEELE. Arrived in Camp 9-30 p.m	M/c
Sheet 27 W.2. 1/40,000 L.13.d.3.4.	23	2 p.m. 4 p.m.	Cleaning and checking Gun Equipment.	M/c M/c
	24	9 a.m.	Inspection and settling into Camp.	M/c
	25.	9 a.m. to 12 a.m. 2 p.m. to 4 p.m.	Barrage Drill, Communication Drill. Gas Drill. Company Inspection, Physical Training, Lecture for N.C.Os.	M/c

Army Form C. 2118.

WAR DIARY
or
INTELLIGENCE-SUMMARY.

125TH MACHINE GUN COMPANY.
AUGUST 1917.

(Erase heading not required.)

Instructions regarding War Diaries and Intelligence Summaries are contained in F.S. Regs., Part II. and the Staff Manual respectively. Title pages will be prepared in manuscript.

Place	Date Aug.	Hour	Summary of Events and Information	Remarks and references to Appendices
FRANCE	26		Church Parade. Ceremonial Parade.	
Sheet 28 L/40,000 L.16.a.9.5.	27.	9 a.m. to 12a.m.	Gas Drill, Digging Emplacements with triangular bases.	
		2 p.m. to 4 p.m.	Cleaning Packsaddlery, Belt filling, overhauling belts.	
	28	8-30 to 9 a.m.	Physical Training.	
		9.15a.m. to 12-15	Gun Drill in Gas helmets, Ammunition Supply, stores etc.	
		2-0 to 4 p.m.	Use of Pack Saddlery (Practical)	
Sheet 28. N.E.1. Sheet 28. N.W.2. 1/10,000	29	8 a.m. 8-30 9-30	Struck Camp. 1st Line Transport proceeded by road to L.16.a.9.5., Rear Company Headquarters. Company Marched to POPERINGHE and entrained. Company detrained at ASYLUM H.12.d. and marched to H.18.d.7.2. and bivouaced.	
	30.	2-0p.m. 6.p.m.	Company relieved 46 Machine Gun Company in line. Advanced Company Headquarters moved to FREZENBURG, A 1065,1085,D.19 b 7575,6590. Nos.1 & 3 Sections relieved 8 guns in front line at D.25.c.9560,8565,4885 L.5.a.3.7. Nos 2 & 4 Sections with 4 guns each took up positions for harrassing fire at I.6.c.9580 (IBEX RESERVE) and c.500 2040 (RUPRECHT FARM).	
L.16.a.9.5	31	4-15 a.m.	Relief reported complete. Harrassing guns fired 3,000 rounds during intermittent enemy artillery action night on ZEVENCOTE, BREMEN REDOUBT. Intermittent enemy artillery action of varying intensity round FREZENBURG, chiefly H.E.5.9 in Sketch of positions. Tactical and Technical Lessons learnt during month. Statement showing strength, casualties etc.	APPENDIX "A" " "B" " "C"

[signature] Capt.

APPENDIX "B"

125TH MACHINE GUN COMPANY.

TACTICAL AND TECHNICAL LESSONS LEARNT DURING THE MONTH ENDING 21/8/17.

1. TACTICAL.
   a. Need for somewhat closer co-ordination between Companies, and with the higher Machine Gun Authorities, with reference to concerted operations such as barrages. Also more information should be accorded to Infantry Battalion Commanders as to what may be expected of Machine Guns and what support Infantry may call for, and by what means. This might be effected by a short lecture delivered to Regimental Officers (as a parade) by the G.M.G.O. or D.M.G.O.

   b. Need of careful instruction by experts in digging semi-permanent emplacements of the "slit" type.

(A query has lately arisen as to whether concrete for Machine Gun Emplacements is an advantage or no. Information is requested please as to whether experiences of other Companies in this matter will be published)

2. TECHNICAL.
   a. Urgent necessity for the issue of more clinometers. At present four are issued for 16 guns, and in the event of a rapid change of elevation it is too much to expect of one officer to put his clinometer/ elevation on four guns with the accuracy and speed required.

   b. Locks should be of better quality.

   c. In some cases the barrel block of the new barrel requires filing in order to avoid No.3 Stoppages. This could be done before issue.

   d. The issue of at least one small discetor per Company - preferably two. A special pattern of the artillery Mark IV. discetor might serve.

   e. Issue of oil compasses in lieu of the Prismatic Marks VI & VII. These should be luminous.

   f. The bubble on the Mark V clinometer should be rendered luminous.

   g. One Clinometer and angle of sight Instrument for H.Q.

   h. The Transport questions are re-mentioned.
      (1) A second G.S. Wagon for Baggage.
      (2) A cooker.

(Signed) R.V. GERY.
O.C. 125th Machine Gun Company.

21/8/17.

APPENDIX "C".

STATEMENT SHOWING STRENGTH OF COMPANY, CASUALTIES ETC.

			Offs.	O.R.
Strength of Company Aug.1st.1917. (including 1 Off. and 18 O.R. Attached)			11	195.
	Offs.	O.R.		
Drafts etc.	1	6	1	6.
			12	201.
To Hospital	2§	7		
Transferred to other M.G. Companies.		5		
To Base under age.		1	2	13.
Strength of Company Aug.31st 1917. (including 1 Off. & 19 O.R. attached)			10.	188.

Numbers to Field Ambulance during month of August 1917. 16 O.R.
Numbers returned from Field Ambulance   7 O.R.
Numbers proceeded on leave during month   11 O.R.
Numbers re-joined from Leave during month.   26 O.R.

§ Lieut. D.F.Larkins.
  2nd.Lieut.I.Jaffe.

HORSES ETC. IN POSSESSION.

	Officer's chargers.	Horses L.D.	Mules.
On Aug.1st.1917.	8 (including 1 Interpreters charger)	41.	4.
evacuated during month.	1	5	-
	7	36	4.
Mules drawn in lieu of horses.			3.
TOTAL.	7	36	7.

CONFIDENTIAL

WAR DIARY

for

125th MACHINE GUN COMPANY,

from

September 1st 1917 to September 30th,1917

Volume IX

Army Form C. 2118.

WAR DIARY
or
INTELLIGENCE SUMMARY.
(Erase heading not required.)

Instructions regarding War Diaries and Intelligence Summaries are contained in F. S. Regs., Part II. and the Staff Manual respectively. Title pages will be prepared in manuscript.

Place	Date	Hour	Summary of Events and Information	Remarks and references to Appendices
FRANCE Map Reference Sheet FREZENBERG 1/10000 28.N.E.1 28.N.W.1 1/20000.	Sep.1		The eight guns in forward system remained in position. Harrasing guns in IBEX RESERVE fired 4000 rounds on selected targets in DELVA FARM, BREMEN REDOUBT, VAMPIR area. 4 guns in C. 30. C.2040 engaged in construction of suitable emplacements	12.
	Sep.2		SQUARE FARM positions heavily shelled by day and night with 5.9 and 4.2. Another position constructed in SQUARE FARM to fire N.E. across front of POMMERN CASTLE. IBEX RESERVE positions heavily shelled 10 p.m. - midnight.	12.
	Sep.3		Fresh positions reconnoitred for IBEX RESERVE guns at CRATER on road C.29 d 3900, and guns moved in at dusk. Guns at RUPPRECHT FARM (C.30 c 2040) came into action firing about 3000 rounds on targets behind IBERIAN, DELVA FARM and in front of ZEVENCOTE. One Horse L.D. and harness accidentally lost.	13
	Sep.4		Two teams of No. 4 Section (L/C Symes and L/C Jennings) and one team of No. 1 Section (L/C Hilton) together with Lieut. R.E.F. Barnett and Sergeant Livsey relieved from front system for rest and preparation for impending offensive. Eight new barrage positions commenced along the line C. 30 d 0545 - C. 30 d 2020, dug and camouflaged. Arrangements commenced for water and ammunition supply. Eight guns of 127th M.G.Company attached to 125th M.G.Company for operations and positions partly dug at C 50 c 88 approximately. Guns at RUPPRECHT FARM continued to fire harrassing fire at night on usual lines. Four guns at CRATER laid on S.O.S. lines but did not fire.	23.

	Sep.5		Usual shelling of SQUARE FARM and positions at G in FREZENBERG, (1/10000 sheet FREZENBERG)
			Lieut. Barnett and the three teams resting returned to from wagon lines and took positions as under
			    Lieut. Barnett "G" in FREZENBERG
			    L/C Symes ditto
			    L/C Jennings ditto
			    Sergeant Livsey ditto
			    Sergeant Dixon POMMERN REDOUBT
				14

Army Form C. 2118.

WAR DIARY
or
INTELLIGENCE SUMMARY.
(Erase heading not required)

Instructions regarding War Diaries and Intelligence Summaries are contained in F. S. Regs., Part II. and the Staff Manual respectively. Title pages will be prepared in manuscript.

Place	Date	Hour	Summary of Events and Information	Remarks and references to Appendices
FRANCE	Sep.6		For operations of these guns see Report "A" appended. Casualties - One mule killed, two other ranks wounded (gas).	A.
			125th Brigade took offensive action against strong points BORRY FARM, BECK HOUSE & IBERIAN, in co-operation with 182nd Brigade attacking Hill 35. 125th Machine Gun Company co-operated with three advancing guns, (see Report "A") and eight on the barrage line C 30 d 0545 - C 30 d 2020, assisted by eight guns of 126 Machine Gun Company on right and 127th Machine Gun Company on left. Casualties to 125th M.G. Company	
			Officers O.R. Killed 7 Died of Wounds 2 Wounded 9 Wounded and missing 1 1 Gassed Material lost-1 gun complete, 2 tripods Mk.IV Belt Boxes	
			2/Lieut. S. Dickinson assumed command of No. 1 Section vice Lieut. R.E.F. Barnett wounded and missing.	
	Sep.7		Left and centre advanced guns relieved in POMMERN and SQUARE FARM respectively by guns of 127th Company. SQUARE FARM and barrage guns also relieved.	A.
	Sep.8		Relief complete 4-20 a.m. Company returned (by train from ASYLUM, YPRES) to BRANDHOEK No. 2 area.	A.
	Sep.9		Company resting and refitting.	A.
	Sep.10		Company inspection, Gas Drill etc. Casualties One other rank to hospital (gas poisoning)	A.

WAR DIARY
or
INTELLIGENCE SUMMARY.
(Erase heading not required.)

Army Form C. 2118.

Place	Date	Hour	Summary of Events and Information	Remarks and references to Appendices
FRANCE	Sep.11		Company resting and refitting	Pg.
	Sep.12		Eight guns under Sergeant Gresty D., D.C.M. and an escort proceeded to CRATER and remained there under orders of O.C. JERK.	Pg.
	Sep.13		Eight guns in CRATER withdrawn under Divisional instructions.	Pg.
	Sep.14		125th Brigade relieved 127th brigade in left sector of Divisional Front. 126th Company relieved 6 guns of 127th Company in front system, dispositions as under G in FRIEZENBERG 2. No. 3 Sect. Capt. Wareham LOW FARM 1. No. 1 Sect. Corp. Wilcox SQUARE FARM 2. No. 2 Sect. 2/Lieut. Dickinson POMMERN REDOUBT 1. No. 1 Sect. Sergeant Dixon 10 guns were also disposed in and around CRATER(C 29 d 3900), four laid on S.O.S. lines, two on anti-aircraft duty and four in reserve. Transport moved from BRANDHOEK No. 2 area to YPRES SOUTH.	Pg.
	Sep.15		Usual artillery activity, otherwise quiet day.	
	Sep.16		CRATER positions shelled in evening. Casualties Killed 2 O.R. Wounded 6 O.R. SQUARE FARM shelled in afternoon. Casualties Wounded 3 O.R.	Pg. Pg.
	Sep.17		CRATER positions again shelled. One gun and tripod hit. Company Headquarters shelled 10 p.m. Casualties Wounded 1 O.R.	Pg.

Army Form C. 2118.

WAR DIARY
or
INTELLIGENCE SUMMARY.
(Erase heading not required.)

Instructions regarding War Diaries and Intelligence Summaries are contained in F.S. Regs., Part II. and the Staff Manual respectively. Title pages will be prepared in manuscript.

Place	Date	Hour	Summary of Events and Information	Remarks and references to Appendices
France	Sep 18		Transport moved from YPRES SOUTH to BRANDHOEK No. 2 Area. 28th Company relieved 125th Company in sector.	19
	Sep 19	2-20 a.m.	Relief complete. Company proceeded (by train from GOLDFISCH CHATEAU) to BRANDHOEK No. 2 Area.	19
	Sep 20		Company proceeded by route march to SCHOOLS KAMP (ST. JAN-TER-BIEZEN area)	19
	Sep 21		Company training, baths and nesting. 2/Lieut. W.A. Harrison reported for duty with the Company and posted to command No. 2 Section.	19
	Sep 21		Company training. Capt. G.C. Kay and 4 O.R. proceeded on special leave to U.K. Lieut. E.B. Carlisle assumed duties of 2nd i/c of the Company.	19
	Sep 22		Company entrained at HOBOUTRE and proceeded to ARNEKE, thence by march route to LEDRINGHEM. Transport moved by road to same area.	19
	Sep 23		Company resting.	19
	Sep 24		Company entrained at ESQUELBEC for GHYVELDE with transport.	24
	Sep 25		Company proceeded by march route to COXYDE BAINS.	29
	Sep 26		Company training, bathing and gas parades.	28
	Sep 27		Company training and bathing.	29
	Sep 28		Company having route march and cleaning camp	28
	Sep 29		Company training	19
	Sep 30		Voluntary church parades.	19

REPORT "A".

The 125th Machine Gun Company took part in Offensive operations in the FREZENBERG Area (East of YPRES) on the 6th September 1917.

Attached hereto :   i. Map of FREZENBERG Area (FREZENBERG 1/10,000-) showing various positions of barrage, stopping and advancing guns.

    ii. Copy 125th Brigade O.O. No.35.

    iii. Copy of 42nd. Divisional Memo of 3rd. September 1917.

    iv. Copy of 125th Brigade Instructions No. 2. attached to 125th Brigade O.O. No.35.

General Idea. The advance of July 31st on the LANGEMARCK - ZONNEBEKE ~~strongpoints~~ Sector had been held up by the enemy stong points just in front of the LANGEMARCK - GHELUVELD line. Sheet 28 J.2.b.69 - Sheet C.12.central).

The enemy method of defence had developed into a number of concreted farmhouses and redoubts to reduce which special and separate treatment by Artillery, gas and infantry assualt was needed.
In order to avoid the necessity of wintering in the valley of the ZONNEBEKE and STEENBEKE it became necessary to make a determined assualt on the line Hill 37 (D.20.d.88) - Hill 35 (D.19c.27), embracing certain strong points in front of and between these.

Special Idea. In order to test the strength of the concrete positions adopted by the enemy as above, the 125th Infantry Brigade was detailed to attack the three points BORRY FARM (D.25.d.) BECK HOUSE (D.19.d.) and IBERIAN (D.19.b.)
These points were to be taken and consolidated against anticipated counter attacks.

Measures for attack.
    i. <u>Artillery.</u> Each of the strong points was previously treated with 15 inch, 12 inch and 6 inch howitzers, and the usual creeping barrage was put down in front of the advancing infantry as in attached programme.
    ii. <u>Gas.</u> Each of the strong Points was treated on Y night with gas from projectors.
    iii. <u>Smoke.</u> Smoke barrages were put out as in attached programme on W, X and Y.
    iv. <u>Machine Gun Barrages.</u> See attached Map.
24 guns (eight of 125th Coy., eight of 126th Coy., eight of 127th Coy) fired as per time table on the line.
Two guns of 125 Company fired direct on to VAMPIR and Hill 35 as per time table.
    v. <u>Infantry</u> Two Companies of Infantry with one gun of 125th Coy., attacked BORRY FARM at zero.
One Company of infantry with one gun of 125th Coy., attacked BECK HOUSE at zero.
One Company of infantry with one gun of 125th Coy., attacked IBERIAN at zero.
    vi. <u>Machine Guns Going Over</u>
Three as above (in para. v.)

125th Inf. Brigade.   M/68.

TACTICAL AND TECHNICAL LESSONS LEARNT.

TACTICAL.

1. Immense advantage of Machine Guns disposed checkerwise in depth, with strong headcover. Also comparative immunity of Machine Guns disposed in shell holes in open.

2. Vital necessity for Infantry Commanders to recognise the psychological moment for calling up consolidation Machine Guns.

3. Necessity for M.G. Barrage Groups to be connected to Brigade Headquarters by some safe means of signalling. Suggestions..
   1. Buried Cable.   2. Pigeons.

4. Very rapid replacement of casualties. Suggested that a reserve of trained Machine Gunners should be kept, if not at Brigade Headquarters, at least at Advanced D.H.Q.
   These to be reinforcements and not taken off the strength of the Companies employed.

TECHNICAL.

1. At least three, if not four, days required for preparing effective barrage positions.
2. At least one Officer and two N.C.Os per Company should attend a camouflage course.
3. The bag trench to be fitted with springs or quick release straps for carrying cleaning rod, etc. and a pocket for cleaning materials.
4. The immediate issue of the new flash concealer to Units.

21-9-17.

Captain.
O.C. 125th Machine Gun Company.

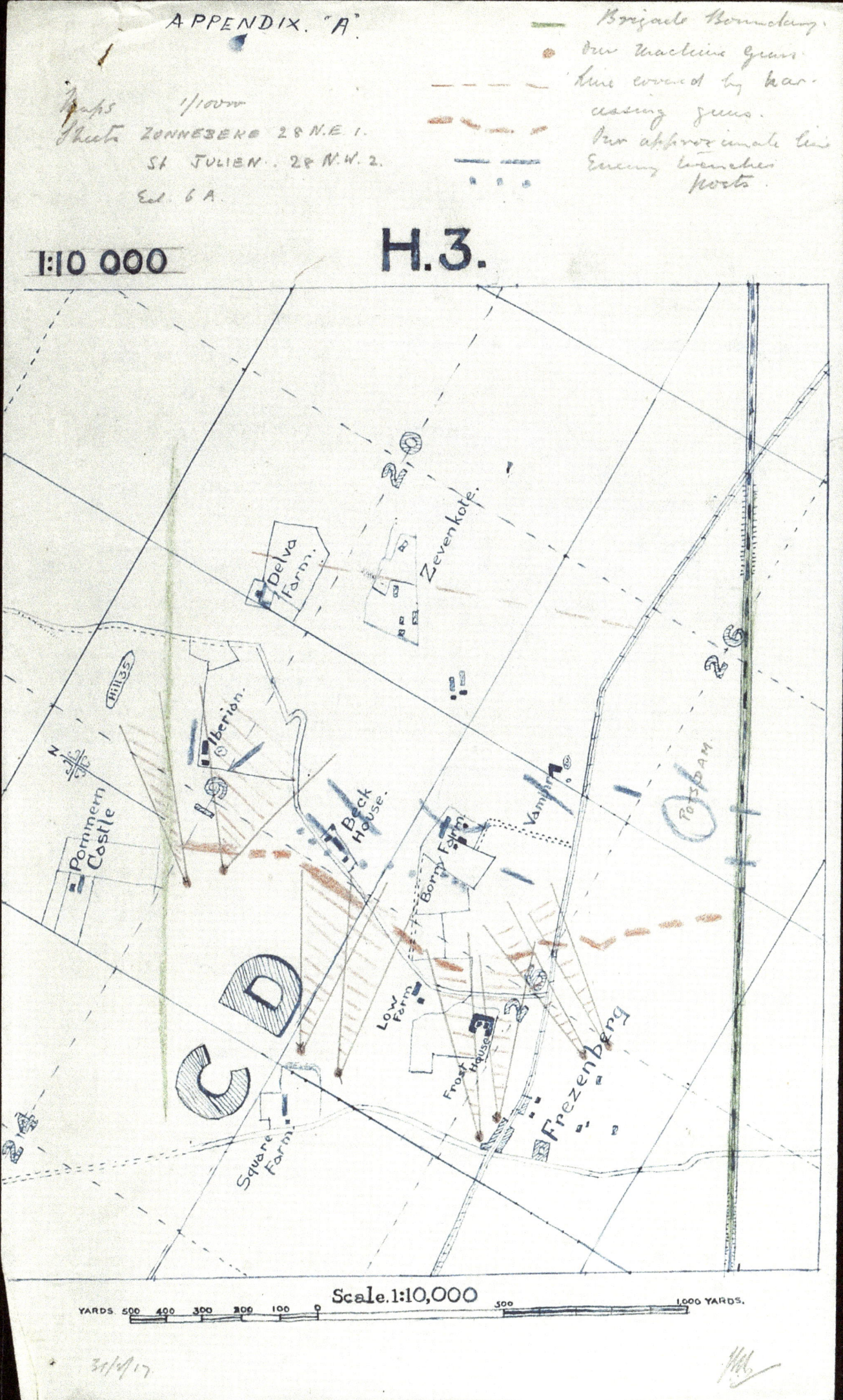

Copy No. 4

MOVE ORDER NO. 7.

BY

CAPTAIN E. V. GERY.

COMMANDING "JANGLE".

Ref. Sheets 27 & 28.
1/40,000.
─────────────

1. THE "JANGLE" will move to YPRES SOUTH area to-morrow by road and rail as shown below.
   When on the march from entraining point an interval of 200 yards will be kept between Sections from detraining points to billets. Transport will parade ready to move off at 8-30 a.m.. Move is to H.16.a.8.4. by road. Starting Point Road Junction L.8.d.8.6. at 9-30 a.m. Dress. Full Marching Order.
   The Company will parade ready to move off at 9-10 a.m. Dress. Full Marching Order. Packs will be worn.

2. A rear party of Sgt. Teal T. and 2 O.R. to be detailed by C.Q.M. will remain behind and obtain a certificate from the Area Commandant that the Camp and Billets were left in a sanitary and clean condition. They will be taken on later by our Lorry which will also take rear parties of 5th and 7th Lan. Fus.

3. A dump for heavy baggage is being formed at 16 PLACE BERTIN, POPERINGHE. Heavy Baggage to be at the Q.M. Stores ready for loading at 8-0 a.m. C.Q.M.Sgt. and 6 men unfit to march (if any) will proceed with Lorry for unloading purposes and will re-join the Company at POPERINGHE, Station as soon as possible (not later than 11-30 a.m.)
   Pte. Nightingale will remain in charge of the dump.

4. WATER BOTTLES will be filled to-night.

5. Oil Cans for the Guns will be filled to-night.

6. Haversack rations will be carried.

7. Officers Valises not exceeding 20 lbs in weight will be taken on the Section Limbers. Remainder to be put in sacks and sent with heavy Baggage.

Issued at 8-30 p.m.
28/6/17.

Copies to :-
1. Off. Mess.
2. Transport Officer.
3. C.Q.M.
4. War Diary
5. File.

Captain.
O.C. "JANGLE".

SECRET.   Copy No. 5.

125th BRIGADE OPERATION ORDER NUMBER 35   4.9.17.

Map Reference FREZENBERG Edition 3, 1/10,000

1. The 125th Brigade will attack and capture the Strong Points in the neighbourhood of BORRY FARM, BECK HOUSE and IBERIAN on "Z" Day.
    The 61st Division is attacking GALLIPOLI on the same day and at the same time.

2. The 5th Lan Fus will attack BORRY with 2 Companies.
    The 7th Lan Fus will attack BECK with 1 Company and IBERIAN 2 Companies.

3. The Table of Artillery Barrage and Gas Bombardment is attached. Barrage Map will be issued later.

4. Instructions for R.E. for consolidation of the Objectives have been issued to all concerned,
    125th BRIGADE INSTRUCTIONS NUMBER 1 dated 3rd inst.

5. Instructions for M.Gs. have been issued to all concerned in 125th BRIGADE INSTRUCTIONS NUMBER 2 dated 4th inst.

6. Instructions for T.M.Battery have been issued to all concerned in 125th BRIGADE INSTRUCTIONS NUMBER 3 dated 4th inst.

7. Dress for assaulting Companies :-
    Go over Kit without Entrenching Tools, Haversacks, Bombs or Flares. Each man will carry the following :-
    - 3 Sandbags
    - 1 Lewis Gun Drum (Lewis Gun Teams will carry the usual number of Drums.
    - 1 Day's rations (In addition to the Iron Ration)
    - 1 Extra Water Bottle (attached on Left Side)
    - 200 Rounds S.A.A.
    - Waterproof Sheet
    - Bombers will carry 8 Bombs a man.
    - Rifle Grenadiers, 6 rifle Grenades each.
    - M.G.Company 1 Day's Rations (In addition to Iron Ration) and an extra Water Bottle.

8. Watches will be Synchronised by an Officer from Brigade Headquarters on "Y" Day.

9. "Z" Day and Zero Hour will be notified later.

10. ACKNOWLEDGE.

                                    (sgd) A.E.Lawrence, Captain
                                             Brigade Major,
                                             125th BRIGADE.

Issued at... a.m. by Signals.
Copies to:-
1. 5th Lan Fus.   11. 42nd Division
2. 6th Lan Fus.   12. Right Sub Group Artillery.
3. 7th Lan Fus.   13. Left Sub Group Artillery.
4. 8th Lan Fus.   14. Special Companies R.E.
5. 125th M.G.Company   15. Brigade Major.
6. 125th T.M.Battery   16. Staff Captain.
7. 126th M.G.Company   17. Signalling Officer.
8. 127th M.G.Company   18) War Diary
9. 126th Brigade   19)
10. 182nd Brigade   20. FILE

TIME TABLE FOR 24 GUNS FIRING

ON LANGEMARCK - GHELUVELT LINE

Zero to Zero Plus 5 minutes. Fire at rate of 1 Belt per 2 minutes

Zero Plus 5 to Zero Plus 15 minutes. Fire at rate of 1 Belt per
                                                                           5 minutes.

Zero plus 15 to Zero plus 40 minutes. Bursts of Fire only.

Zero Plus 40 minutes to Zero Plus 10 Hours. Stand by and look out
                                                                   for S.O.S. Signals.

APPENDIX

STATEMENT SHOWING STRENGTH OF COMPANY, CASUALTIES ETC.

	Offs.	O.R.
Strength of Company Sept. 1st.1917. (including 2 offs. & 15 O.R.)	10	188.
Drafts etc.	2	62.
	12.	250.

Casualties.	Offs.	O.R.		
Killed.	-	8		
Died of wounds.	-	3.		
Wounded.	-	19.		
Wounded (Gas)	-	2.		
Wounded & missing	1	1.		
	1	33.		
Hospital		4.	1.	37.
Strength at 30th Sept.1917. (Including 2 Offs. & 15 O.R. attached)			11.	213.

Numbers to Field Ambulance during month of Sept.	16 O.R.
Numbers re-joined from Field Ambulance	10.O.R.
Numbers proceeded on Leave during month.	8.O.R.
Numbers re-joined from Leave during month.	6 O.R.

HORSES ETC. IN POSSESSION.

	Officers Chargers.	Horses L.D.	Mules.
On Sept.1st. 1917.	7	36	7.
evacuated during month.			
Killed, 1 mule			2.
Wounded. 1 mule.			
	7	36	5.
Animals drawn during month.	1	2	7
Present Strength.	8.	38	12.

Results of Operations

BORRY FARM   The Infantry got within 100 yards of their objective, but were then met with heavy machine gun fire from direction of VAMPIR and BREMEN REDOUBT. The going over gun was called up from its jumping off position (G in FREZENBERG) but was put out of action by a direct hit on the tripod, the sergeant in charge being killed. The remainder of the team succeeded in extricating the gun on the Infantry withdrawing.

BECK HOUSE   The Infantry captured BECK HOUSE soon after zero and the going over gun moved up to consolidate. Lieut. R.E.F. Barnett, who was in charge of this party was severely wounded during consolidation, but the team got the gun mounted in a shell hole and with the help of a captured German gun repelled a counter attack observed to be massing in front of of BREMEN.

A second counter attack however, forced the infantry to withdraw with heavy losses: the gun being left in position. Three of the team withdrew with information to SQUARE FARM.

IBERIAN   This gun did not advance, owing to the Infantry being held up by M.G. fire from Hill 35.

Casualties   Killed   7
                Wounded   9
                Died of wounds   2
                Wounded & missing 2

30.9.17

Captain
O.C. 125 M.G. Coy.

125th Inf. Bde.
126th Inf. Bde.
127th Inf. Bde.

During the operation of the 6th inst. it is proposed to use 8 Machine Guns from each M.G. Company in the Division in giving covering fire directed on to the LANGEMARK - CHELUVELT Line.

Locations of these batteries and their zones of fire are indicated on the attached map.

Company Commanders should reconnoitre exact positions to be occupied by their Batteries at once.

Suggested time table and rate of fire of these guns is attached.

In addition to the covering fire referred to it is desired to keep the following points under direct Machine Gun fire

From Zero hour to plus 10 Minutes

By 125th Machine Gun Company, line of Railway from D.26 c.4 to D.26 b.2.0., Area around POTSDAM and BIT WORK., Road at point D.19.b.9.8 (M.G. nest).

By 126th Machine Gun Company, ZONNEKE REDOUBT., BRIDGE and CONCRETE SHELTER at D.26b.2.0

Rate of fire suggested for above :-

From Zero Hour to Plus 10 Minutes - 1 Belt per 3 minutes

3rd Sept. 1917.

Lt. Colonel,
General Staff,
42nd. Division.

TIME TABLE FOR 24 GUNS FIRING ON TO LANGEMARK-GHELUVELT Line.

From	Zero hour to Plus 5 Minutes	Fire at rate of 1 belt per 2 minutes.
From	Zero plus 5 to plus 15	Fire at rate of 1 belt per 5 minutes.
"	" " 15 " " 40	Bursts of fire only.
"	" " 40 " " 10 Hrs.	Stand by and look out for S.O.S. Signal.

At Zero Plus 10 Hours at the discretion of B.G's.C. Brigades, all extra guns brought up for barrage work can dismiss.

80,000 rounds S.A.A. for Machine Guns will be delivered at BAVARIA HOUSE to-night, 3/4th September.

Tasks are allotted to each Company as shewn in various colours on attached Map.

SECRET.   Copy No.5.

125th BRIGADE INSTRUCTIONS NUMBER 2.   4/9/17.

Ref.Map FREZENBERG 1/10,000.

INSTRUCTIONS FOR MACHINE GUNS IN ATTACK.
ON BORRY, BECK AND IBERIAN.

1. 24 guns (8 from each M.G.Company in the Division) will bring covering fire direct on to the LANGEMARCK - GHELUVELT Line. Locations of these batteries and their Zones of Fire are shown on the attached Map.

   125th M.G.Company.   BLUE.
   126th M.G.Company.   BROWN.
   127th M.G.Company.   RED.

   Time Table and Rate of Fire attached.

2. From Zero to Zero plus 10 minutes.

   The following Points will be kept under direct M.G.Fire :-
                                    M.G.
          By 125th Company   BLUE.

   Line of the railway from D.26.c.1.4. to D.26.b.2.0.; the area around POTSDAM and BITWORK and the Road at D.19.b.9.8.

          By 126th M.G.Company.   BROWN.

   ZONNEBEKE REDOUBT and the Bridge and concrete shelter at D.26.b.2.0.   Rate of Fire One Belt per 3 Minutes.

3. O.C.125th M.G.Company will arrange for one Gun to go over to each Objective as soon as it is ascertained that it has been captured.

(a) BORRY
        The gun and Team will be at FROST HOUSE.
        O.C.5th Lan.Fus.will arrange to inform this Gun when to move.

(b) BECK.
        The Gun and Team will be at FROST HOUSE.
        O.C.6th Lan.Fus. will arrange to inform this Gun when to move.

(c) IBERIAN.
        The Gun and Team will be at D.19.c.7.9.
        O.C. 6th Lan.Fus will arrange to inform this Gun when to move.

4. O.C.7th Lan.Fus. will detail 12 men to act as carrying Parties (4 Men for each Gun). They will report to O.C. 125th M.G.Company at noon on "Y" Day.

5. O.C. 125th M.G.Company will, in conference with Os.C. 5th and 6th Lan Fus arrange to place his remaining five Guns to form a screen across our present Front Line should the enemy Counter Attack.

6. A C K N O W L E D G E.
                              (sgd)   A E Lawrence, Captain,
                                            Brigade Major,
                                            125th BRIGADE.

Issued to :-

1. 5th Lan Fus.   x
2. 6th Lan Fus.   x
3. 7th Lan Fus.
4. 8th Lan Fus.
5. 125th M.G. Company
6. 126th M.G. Company
7. 125th T.M. Battery
8. 127th M.G. Company
9. 126th Brigade
10. 182nd Brigade
11. 42nd Division
12. M.G. Officer, 42nd Division.

    x   Maps issued

CONFIDENTIAL.

WAR DIARY

FOR

125th MACHINE GUN COMPANY,

FROM

OCTOBER 1st., 1917   TO   OCTOBER 31st., 1917.

———VOLUME X.———

Army Form C. 2118.

WAR DIARY
INTELLIGENCE SUMMARY
(Erase heading not required.)

125th Company M.G.C.

OCTOBER 1917

Place	Date 1917	Hour	Summary of Events and Information	Remarks and references to Appendices
Map. Ref. FURNES 1/40000 W.S.d.Central	Oct 1	8.30am-12.15pm	Physical Training, Close order drill, Barrage drill, Bathing	
	"	2-4.40 pm	Transport Inspection. Sections at disposal of Section officers.	
	" 2.	9am	Demonstration of Right and Smoke Signals	
		2pm	Revolver Practice.	
	"		The following were awarded the Military Medal:- 69607 Pte (A/L/Cpl Jennings J., 39487 Sergt Dixon a., 39592 Pte Broadhurst R., 39603 Pte Bromley C.	
	" 3	8.30-12.15pm	Physical Training, Close order & Combined drill & Bathing	
	"	2pm-4pm	Barrage Practice on Range	
	"		2.O.R. to 4th Army Mobile Workshop. Lieut Clymer JA. & 2.O.R. returned from 1st Gas Course.	
	"		Divisional School. 1 O.R. from hospital. 3.O.R. taken on strength	
	" 4	9-12.15pm	Elementary Drill, Immediate action, Bathing	
	"	2-4pm	Revolver Practice on Range	
	"		Capt. G. C. Kay rejoined from leave to U.K.	
	" 5	9-12.15pm	Route March :- Company less Transport St IDESBALDE, DE ZEPANNE, KERKPANNE, LA PANNE, ADINKERKE, OOSTHOEK. W.23.C.8.O. W.22.6.14.7. KERKPANNE & back to billets.	
	"		2.O.R. proceeded to 6th Course A.H.T.D. ABBEVILLE. 3.O.R. returned from leave.	

Army Form C. 2118.

WAR DIARY
of
INTELLIGENCE SUMMARY.
(Erase heading not required.)

125 Company M.G.C.

OCTOBER 1917

Place	Date 1917	Hour	Summary of Events and Information	Remarks and references to Appendices
Map.Ref. FURNES. 1/40000 W.S.A CENTRAL.	Oct. 6	9. am	Ceremonial Parade: Packing limber.	
		2. pm	Company evacuated billets and moved to AUSTRALIA CAMP. W.18.a.55.	
		5. pm	Company relieved 97th Machine Gun Company in the NIEUPORT SECTOR night 6/7th Relief complete 11 p.m.	APPENDIX "A" Relief Orders. APPENDIX "IXB"
Map. No.5 NIEUPORT 1/10000	" 7		Copy of Relief Order attached. Appendix attached containing maps showing positions & lines of fire & tables of calculations. 2 guns No.2 Section fired 2000 rounds harassing fire from M.29.a.o.o. on M.17.c.15.00. & M.16.d.6520 during the night. 2 guns No.4 Section fired 2000 rounds harassing fire from M.28.c.147.2 & 1173 on M.16.d.7545 & M.17.c.3407.	
	" 8		2 guns of No.2 Section searched M.17.c.15 & M.10.d.6520 during the night from M.29.a.0008, 2000 rounds were fired. 2 guns of No.4 section defensive from M.28.c.2290 & 1596 on M.17.c.0020 & M.17.a.2515. 2000 rounds were fired. No.1. Section 127th M.G.Co. on PRESQUILE was relieved by No.4 Section.	
	" 9		2 guns No.2 Section & 2 guns No.4 Section each fired 2000 rounds during the night from their harassing fire positions on M.18.c.57, M.18.a.6525, M.17.d.7570, M.17.c.5095. Gun position at M.28.c.1472 was blown in by a shell.	

Army Form C. 2118.

WAR DIARY

INTELLIGENCE SUMMARY.
(Erase heading not required.)

125 Company M.G.C.

OCTOBER 1917

Place	Date 1917	Hour	Summary of Events and Information	Remarks and references to Appendices
No.5 NIEUPORT. 1/1000D	Oct 10		No. 4 Section worked on new harassing fire positions, and fixed anti-aircraft mounting at M.27.d.4555. 2 guns No.2 Section fired 2000 rounds during night on M.17.c.8040 & M.17.A.4040. 2 guns No.4 Section at M.28.c.1607 & M.28.a.0901 fired 2000 rounds Sifting fire on the same targets. Capt. G.S. Wrockham transferred to 13th M.G. Coy. 2nd I/C.	M.C.
	" 11		2 guns No.2 Section fired 2000 rounds during night on M.18.c.0234 or 18.a.3656. 2/Lieut. 107A Stranson to Field Amb. 2/Lieut. W.N. Stranson (4 Lincoln T.F.) M.G.C., posted to Company. I.O.R. Leave to U.K.	M.C.
	" 12		Working Party of 1 N.C.O. and 16 men supplied from wagon lines to No.4 Section for work on PRESQUILE deepening trenches, etc. Lieut. Wm.S. BREIDFJORD took over No. 2 Section from Sergt. TURNER. Anti-aircraft gun fire 160 at hostile aeroplane about 9. a.m. 2 guns No.2 Section fired 2000 rounds during night at M.17.a.6005 & M.17.c.0236. Lieut. H.A.SALE & I.O.R. proceeded to XVth Corps Infantry School for a course. I.O.R. to 3rd Divisional Gas School. (Course).	M.C.
	" 13		Anti-Aircraft gun fired 500 rounds during morning at hostile aircraft. 2 guns No.2 Section fired 2000 rounds on M.17.a.6003 & 9565.	M.C.

Army Form C. 2118.

WAR DIARY
~~INTELLIGENCE SUMMARY~~
(Erase heading not required.)

125 Company M.G.C.

OCTOBER 1917

Instructions regarding War Diaries and Intelligence Summaries are contained in F. S. Regs., Part II. and the Staff Manual respectively. Title pages will be prepared in manuscript.

Place	Date 1917	Hour	Summary of Events and Information	Remarks and references to Appendices
NO. 5 NIEUPORT. 1/10000.	Oct. 14		No. 4 Section built new emplacements at M.27.b.8050 & M.27.b.9527	
			2 guns No. 2 Section, fired 2000 rounds as usual on M.17.c.0234 & 1552.	
			Capt. G.C. KAY proceeded to Advanced Company H.Q.	
	" 15		2 guns No. 2 section fired 2000 rounds searching round M.28.c.0234 & M.17.c.1552 during the night.	
	" 16		No firing. CAPT. GERY proceeded to wagon lines.	
	" 17		2 guns of No. 4 Section fired from M.28.c.2290 & 1587. 2000 rounds during night, in retaliation for shelling on M.17.a.0758 & M.17.c.8085.	
			CAPT. G.C. KAY & Lt. CLYMER went up to front line for S.O.S. line tests. The clearance over front line was satisfactory.	
			Sergt. 45.W. WILCOX & Sergt. H. SMITH, proceeded to M.G.T.C., GRANTHAM, for a special course of instruction. I.O.R. L.S.H. Bn'l Gas Course.	
	" 18	8 P.m.	No. 2 Section relieved No 4 Section, 127 M.G. Coy on the PRESQUILE.	RELIEF ORDER APPENDIX "C"
			No. 4 section completed emplacement at M.27.b.9431.	
			Anti Aircraft Gun fired 300 rounds at hostile aeroplanes.	
			2 guns No. 4 Section fired a 1000 rounds, special strafe 6 to 7 p.m. on M.17.c.1552 & M.17.a.9563	

Army Form C. 2118.

WAR DIARY
INTELLIGENCE SUMMARY.
(Erase heading not required.)

125 Company M.G.C.

OCTOBER 1917

Place	Date 1917	Hour	Summary of Events and Information	Remarks and references to Appendices
No 5 NIEUPORT 1/10,000	Oct. 18		Coles firing 2000 rounds harassing fire during the night on M.17.a.6520.	M.K.
	"19		Anti-Aircraft gun fired 500 rounds at enemy planes. Special "strafe" as previous night repeated, & thought to have been effective owing to enemy searching for the machine guns. 2 guns No.4 section fired 2000 rounds during night on M.17.a.9363 & 8550	M.K.
	"20		2 guns No. 4 section harassed M.17.a.4062 & M.17.a.8520 .. 2000 rounds. Sergt Turner proceeded to U.K. to Cadet Battalion for a Commission. 4 guns, 11th M.M.G.o., relieved No 2 Section on PRESQUILE at 4 am. Work done on gun position & improving approaches. 1.O.R. wounded.	RELIEF ORDERS APPENDIX "D" M.K. M.K.
	"21.		Anti-Aircraft gun fired 500 rounds at hostile aeroplanes. 2 guns No.4 section fired 2000 rounds during night on M.17.a.4062 & M.17.a.8520	M.K.
	"22		2 guns No 4 section fired 2000 rounds during night on M.17.a.4062 & M.17.a.8520.	M.K.
	"23		The 2 guns fired on as the previous evening. 2000 rounds.	M.K.
FURNES 1/40000 W.17.d.55			3 Sections of 125 Machine Gun Coy. were relieved by 3 Sections 127 Machine Gun Coy. during the early morning, returning to AUSTRALIA CAMP. Relief complete 5-30 am.	RELIEF ORDERS APPENDIX "E" M.K.

Army Form C. 2118.

WAR DIARY
INTELLIGENCE SUMMARY
(Erase heading not required.)

125 Company. M.G.C.

OCTOBER 1917

Instructions regarding War Diaries and Intelligence Summaries are contained in F. S. Regs., Part II. and the Staff Manual respectively. Title pages will be prepared in manuscript.

Place	Date 1917	Hour	Summary of Events and Information	Remarks and references to Appendices
FURNES I/40220 W.18d.55	Oct.23	4 p.m.	Bathing Parade.	fff.
	" 24	9–12.15 a.m.	Cleaning of guns, equipment & inspection	
		2 p.m–4 p.m	Lieut M.A.S. BREIDFJORD & 2.O.R. proceeded to 5th Div'l Gas Course. 1.O.R. returned from leave	fff.
	" 25	8.15–12.15 a.m.	Cleaning and overhauling belts & ammunition. Kit inspections	
		2.4 p.m	Lieut. A.L. HERRIDGE and 3.O.R. proceeded to 1st Anti-Aircraft Course XV Corps School	fff.
	" 26	9.30–12.15 a.m.	Company Inspection. Care & handling of revolvers. Elementary Gun Drill.	fff.
		2–4 p.m	Immediate Action and Stoppages	fff.
	" 27	10 a.m.	Company Inspection. Marching Order.	fff.
	" 28		Church Parade. Lieut A.L. HERRIDGE & 3.O.R. returned from Anti-Aircraft Course.	fff.
	" 29	8.30–12.15 a.m.	Physical Training; washing & cleaning limbers	
		2–4 p.m	Care & handling of revolvers; overhauling guns and spare parts. 5. O.R. proceeded on leave to U.K. 2/Lieut. W.N. STRAWSON & 3.O.R. proceeded to 2nd Anti-Aircraft Course XV Corps School.	fff.
	" 30	9.0–12.15 a.m.	Cleaning and oiling limbers	
		2.0–4 p.m	Stoppages and Immediate Action	
			Lieut M.A.S. BREIDFJORD & 2.O.R. returned from Div'l Gas Course; 1.O.R. to hospital	fff.

Army Form C. 2118.

WAR DIARY
INTELLIGENCE SUMMARY

125 Company M.G.C.

OCTOBER 1917

(Erase heading not required.)

Instructions regarding War Diaries and Intelligence Summaries are contained in F. S. Regs., Part II. and the Staff Manual respectively. Title pages will be prepared in manuscript.

Place	Date 1917	Hour	Summary of Events and Information	Remarks and references to Appendices
MAP REF. FURNES 1/40000 55 W18A Central	Oct. 30	2.4 p.m.	2/Lieut S. DICKINSON & 2.O.R. returned from M.G. School, CAMIERS	
			2.O.R. returned from Transport Course, ABBEVILLE.	
	" 31	10.am	B.G.C. Inspected Company.	
			6. O.R. on Leave to U.K; 1.O.R. to Veterinary Course NEUFCHATEL; 1.O.R. to 6th Div'l Gas Course	
			The following are attached	
			Copy of report on 'Tactical & Technical Reconnaissance' during the month	Appendix F.
			Copy of 'Suggestions re organisation of Machine Gun Companies'.	Appendix G.
			A statement showing strength of the Company during the month.	Appendix H.

31/10/17

Wing
Captain
Commanding 125 M.G. Coy

Appendix A.

SECRET.

RELIEF ORDERS BY CAPTAIN,

R. V. GERY,

COMMANDING " R A I N "

In the Field,
6th October 1917.

Ref. Map 1/20,000.
Belgium Sheet 12 S.W.
_____

1. RAIN will relieve 97th Machine Gun Company in the NIEWPORT SECTOR on night 6/7th October

2. 16 Guns will be relieved. Fourteen belts per gun will be taken over, in the line and equivalent number being handed over by 2nd in Command to 2nd in Command, 97th Company at AUSTRALIA CAMP, COXYDE.

3. Guns in the line will be grouped in 4 Groups) A,B,C and D. Dispositions will be notified to Group Commanders.
   Each Group will number its guns from the right.

   "A" Group No. 2 Section, under Command of Sgt. Turner W R.
   "B" & "C" Groups, Nos 1 & 3 Sections - under Command of Capt. C.S.
   Wareham with Lt. J.A. Clymer.
   "D" Group No. 4 Section - under Command of Lt. A.L.Herridge.

   Company Headquarters, Capt. R.V.Gery & Capt. H.B.Carlisle.

4. The following will be at Advanced Company Headquarters:-
   2 Officers, 2 Batmen, C.S.M. 4 Signallers (including 1 Cpl.) detailed by Cpl. Dixon), 1 Cook,(Farrar), 1 Orderly Room Clerk, (LCpl. Denton.)

5. The Company will parade at 9 am. for packing limbers. Each Section will pack 4 guns, 4 tripods, spare parts, Condensers, Auxiliary tripods, oil etc. Greatcoats, 4 petrol cans filled and one day's rations - in one Limber.
   Each Section will repack its second fighting limber with the remainder of its stores.
   Sections will hand in 14 belts (filled in boxes) per gun, to Q.M. stores before repacking their second limber, except No. 1 Section which will hand in 14 boxes per gun for 3 guns and 4 boxes for the 4th.
   Headquarter Limber will be packed with eight aiming posts, 4 petrol tins, filled, Orderly Room papers etc. to go into the line, two telephones and wire, two Officers' kits and rations for 12 men.
   Sergt. Gandy will superintend the packing of this Limber.

6. 11 am. Inspection of Anit-Gas Appliances by Gas N.C.Os.

7. All men going up the line will hand in their packs to Q.M.Stores by 2 p.m.

8. The Company will parade in full marching order,(filled water bottles) by Sections, complete with Transport at 5.p.m. and will move via OOST-DUNKERKE AND ZOUAVE TRACK, to "T" Roads (Map reference M.34.c.4.0.), head of column arriving at this point at 7 p.m.
   Artillery Formation will be adopted North East of OOST-DUNKERKE, (i.e. 500 yards distances between Sections and Transport).

9. Three men a gun (exclusive of Nos. 1 already in line)will go into the line.

10. C.S.M. will detail one man not going up into the line per limber as brakesman.

Captain,
O.C., 125th Machine Gun Company.

Appendix B.

M.G. Form "B".

125th Co^y S.O.S. Lewis MACHINE GUN BARRAGE FIRE.

~~Group~~ No. ~~Barrage~~. Date Oct. 20th 1917. Map used 1.a.5. NIEUPORT 1:20. Your O.C. Group 11th Carlisle Coft.

Gun No. and Map Location.	Range to Barrage Line in Yards.	ELEVATION			Q.E. in Minutes. Tables 3(a) or 3(b)	Range Yards. Corresponding to Q.E. Table 1, Col. 2.	CLEARANCE OVER OWN TROOPS. (To be worked out for each lift.)					DIRECTION.	REMARKS.		
		Contours in Yards. Gun. A.	Barrage Line.	V.L. in Yards.			Contour of own Troops in Yards. B.	Range to own Troops in Yards.	Traj. Height in Yards. Table 2. C.	Clearance obtained by Note (1) below.	Clearance required in Yards.	Grid Bearing.	Firing. From	To	Rounds.	Checked by.	General.
F4. M29a 6576	Close defence guns.												At visible target				250 r.p.m. = 250 rounds per minute. 50 r.p.m.
Y5. M13d 6464.	do.												do.				Occasional bursts about
Y6. M.23d 6171.	do.												do.				this reg.
Y7a. M28b 4030.	do.												do.				All indirect fire
Y7. M28b 4030																
Y7b. M28a 9360 M17a 5504	1950	4	7	3	246	1950	6	1000	48	46	20	25°	S.O.S.G. S.O.S.+ to 1. 250 r.p.m.	do.			Traverse 1° right
Y8. M28a 5905	Close defence gun												S.O.S.+ to 10. twenty. 50 r.p.m. occasional.				
Y8a. M28a 5303 M17a 4715	2250	4	1	1	341	2250	6	1300	90	88	31	26°	At visible target	do.			Traverse 1° right
Y9. M28a 0601 M13a 9975	2000	3	5	2	260	2000	3	1500	53	53	40	45°	S.O.S.G. S.O.S.+to 10. 250 r.p.m. occasional. 1 left.	do.			
Y9a. M28a 0440 M13a 3080	1800	3	5	2	206	1800	3	1400	34	34	35	40°		do.			
Y9. M27b 9527 M17c 1532	2000	3	5	2	260	2000	3	1300	59	59	31	34½°		do.			
Y10. M27b 9431 M17c 0060	2000	3	5	2	260	2000	3	1300	59	59	31	33°		do.			
Y11. M21d 6140 M23b 8590	2300	5	5	1	360	2300	5	1200	96	96	27	71°		do.			
Y11c M23b 6057	1950	5	5	1	242	1950	5	1200	54	54	27	72°		do.			
Y11a. M21d 5063 M16c 5065	1150	5	5	1	80	1150	}	for friendly troops in the line of fire				27°	At visible target	do.			
Y11a. M21d 4523 M15d 8530	650	5	5	1	31	650						15°	do.				
Y1. M21d 4523 M15d 8530	800	5	5	1	43	800						15°					

NOTES.—(1) Clearance in yards equals A minus B plus or minus C according as trajectory tables give positive or negative values of C.
(2) Immediately before firing Q.E. must be corrected, if necessary, for atmospheric influences. See Table 5.
(3) For lateral wind allowance. See Table 4.
(4) If obstruction exists between gun and target, and its highest point cannot be seen, ascertain if shots will clear by substituting "obstruction" for "own troops" in clearance column above, and find clearance by rule in Note (1). Minimum clearance required equals half height of cone for range to obstruction.

4th Field Survey Coy., R.E. 1633 27-7-17

[P.T.O.

Appendix C.

SECRET. Order No. I. Copy No. 3.

Relief Orders
by
Captain G. C. Kay.
Commanding 125 M. G. Coy.

In the Field
Oct. 17th 1917

1. No. 2 Section will relieve No. 4 Section 127 M.G.Coy. on the PRESQUILE on the morning of the 18th inst.

2. Guides will be met at ROSE VILLA at 3-30 a.m.
Relief will commence 4-0 a.m.
No. 2 Section will be complete in their position with guns mounted and laid on S.O.S. lines by 5 a.m.

3. All Trench Stores, ammunition, range cards etc will be taken over on relief and a list sent to Coy. H.Q. by 7 p.m. Also 8 belt boxes per gun.

4. A carrying party of an N.C.O. and 6 men will report at Coy. H.Q. at 2-30 a.m. to assist No. 2 Section.
They will not return to their dug-outs until being dismissed by O.C. No. 2 Section after completion of the relief and report again with all their kit to Coy. H.Q. at 10-0 a.m. reporting that their dug-outs have been left in a clean and sanitary condition.

5. The ration limbers to-night 17/18th. inst. will collect 32 boxes with belts and ammunition at Coy. H.Q. The Transport Officer will arrange to hand these over and get a receipt from O.C. 127 M.G.Coy.

O.C. No2 Section will report Relief Complete by the Code word "K.O.K"

(Signed) G. C. Kay Capt.
O.C. 125 M.G. Coy.

Appendix D.

SECRET.   Order No. 2.   Copy No. 4.

by

Capt. G.C.Kay

Commanding 125 M.G.Coy.

———————

Ref. Map 1/10,000 No.5.

1. No.2.Section will be relieved by the IIth. M.M.G. Battery on the morning of the 20th inst.

2. Pte Seigal will meet the IIth M.M.G. Battery at the BRIDGE OF SIGHS (M.33b.80.38) at 1-45 a.m. and guide them to ROSE VILLA (M.27b.50.27) arriving there at 3-0 a.m.

3. O.C.No.2.Section will detail one guide for each gun team (II7-II7a II7b & II Yc) and one for Section H.Q. to be at ROSE VILLA at 3-0a.m. These guides will guide each gun team and Section H.Q. into their positions.

   Relief to commence 4 a.m.

   No.2.Section to be clear by 5 a.m.

4. On their arrival at ROSE VILLA on the way out Pte. Seigal will meet and guide No.2.Section via BRIDGE OF SIGHS to where motors placed at their disposal by O.C.IIth. M.M.G. Battery will be waiting for them. He will then return to Coy. H.Q..

   O.C. No.2.Section will report relief complete by the code word "K.O.K" through Pte Seigal.

5. 14 Belt Boxes per gun all trench Stores ammunition, range cards, reserve rations etc. will be handed over on relief and receipt obtained, a copy of which should be sent to Coy.H.Q. by 8.p.m.

6. On and after the night of the 20/21st. inst. the Transport Officer will arrange to convey water and rations for IIth M.M.G. Battery to Coy. H.Q. These rations will be brought to AUSTRALIA CAMP W 18 d 55 by IIth M.M.G. Battery transport and ration carrying parties belonging to IIth M.M.G. Battery should be at Coy. H.Q. to draw them by 6 p.m. each evening.

7. O.C.No.2.Section will hand over all instructions with reference to reports, Intelligence etc. which will be rendered to Coy.H.Q. as heretofore.

Appendix D.

8. A carrying party of 4 men will be detailed by the Sergeant Major. They will accompany Pte Seigal and assist IIth M.M.G. Battery to carry gun tackle in and No.2 Section to bring it out.

    They will return to Coy. H.Q. with Pte Seigal after completing their task.

                     (Signed) G.C. Kay Capt.
                       Commanding 125 M.G. Coy.

Appendix E.

SECRET.   Order No.3.   Copy No.5.

by

Capt. G.C.Kay

Commanding 125 M.G.Coy.

1. Nos. 1,3 &4 Sections 127 M.G.Coy. will relieve 1,3 & 4 Sections 125 M.G.Coy. in the line on the night of the 22/23 Oct.

    No.1. Section 127 M.G.Coy. will relieve
    " 1. " 125 "
    " 3. " 127 " " "
    " 3. " 125 "
    " 4. " 127 " " "
    " 4. " 125 "

2. <u>Detail of relief.</u> Guides etc, will be issued later.

    The following administrative instructions will be followed.

    (a) A & B groups will hand over 14 belts and boxes complete per gun.

    (b) C group hand over 8 belts and boxes complete per gun.

    (c) The number boards on each position (issued tomorrow) will be handed over also all petrol tins in excess of establishment, S.A.A., Grenades etc, maps, photographs, Gas orders, all trench stores etc., receipts to be obtained in duplicate.

    (d) All gum boots will be handed over in as dry a condition as possible and receipts obtained in duplicate.

3. Officers commanding Sections will ensure that lines of fire and all tactical information <u>in writing</u> are handed over correctly and that emplacements, the trenches in the vicinity, dug-outs, H.Q.s. and all accomodation is left in a clean and tidy condition and report to this effect by 12 noon Oct.23rd.

4. One gun number per team of 127 M.G.Coy. will report to O.C. A.B.& C. groups on the 22nd. inst. He will be sent to the position his team is to occupy at dusk or where practicable before and will remain there. No.1 to hand over all position stores and obtain a receipt from this man and give him all possible information about the position, object, and line of fire of the gun.

Capt.

Cmdg. 125 M.G.Coy.

Appendix E.

SECRET.   Order No. 4   Copy No. 8
                        by
                    Capt. G.C.Kay
                Commanding 125 M.G.Coy.
                    ─────────

Reference 1/10000. Sheet 5 Ed. 3   October 21st 1917

1. RELIEF.   The 125 M.G.Coy. (less one section) will be relieved by the
              127 M.G.Coy. (less one section) in the line on the morning
              of the 23rd inst.

2. DETAIL (a) No 1 section 127 M.G.Coy (relieving No. 1 Section 125 M.G.Coy.
              will be at T cross roads at 1-45 a.m.
                 Pte Rowley will be at T cross roads at 1-45 a.m. and will
              conduct this Section and limber to Coy H.Q.
                 O.C. No.1.Section will detail 5 guides, one for each gun
              team and one for section H.Q. to be at Coy. H.Q. by 1-30 a.m.
              to meet the relieving teams and Section H.Q. there, and
              conduct them to their respective positions.
                 The two Lewis Gunners (5 L.F.) with their gun
              ammunition drums etc will be relieved with Y 5 team and will
              accompany No.1. Section back to Wagon lines.
                           ─────────

   (b) No.3.Section 127 M.G.Coy (relieving No.3 Section 125 M.G.Coy.)
              will be at "T" Cross roads at 2-45 a.m.
                 Pte Rowley will be at the "T" Cross Roads at 2-30 a.m.
              and will conduct this Section and limber to Coy.H.Q.
                 O.C.No.3 Section will detail 5 guides, one for each gun
              team and one for Section H.Q. to be at Coy.H.Q. by 2-30 a.m.
              to meet the relieving teams and Section H.Q. there and
              conduct them to their respective positions.
                           ─────────

   (c) No.4.Section 127 M.G.Coy. (relieving No.4.Section 125 M.G.Coy)
              willbe at "T" Cross Roads at 3-30 a.m.
                 Pte.Seigal will be at the "T" Cross Roads at 3-15 a.m.
              and will conduct this Section and limber to ROSE VILLA
                 O.C. No.4 Section will arrange guides here as in the case
              of Nos. 1.&3 Sections.
                           ─────────

Appendix E.

3. GUIDES. Each gun team guide will know the Corps number of his gun position as marked on the position number board so as to be able to pick up the team detailed for his position without any confusion.

---

4. TRANSPORT. The Transport Officer will arrange to have two full limbers at the "T" Cross roads at 5-45 p.m. Oct. 22nd. Pte Myers will meet these limbers and conduct them to Coy. H.Q. to transport H.Q. stores back to the Wagon lines.

He will further arrange to have one limber at Coy. H.Q. at 3-30 a.m. to convey gun tackle etc of No.1. Section and another limber at Coy. H.Q. at 4-30 am. to convey gun tackle of No.3. Section

These limbers will both be met by Pte. Mills (who will guide them to Coy. H.Q.) at "T" Cross Roads at 3-15 a.m. and 4-15 a.m. respectively.

The Transport Officer will further arrange to have a limber at the "T" Cross Roads at 4 a.m. Pte Parsons will meet the limber and guide it to ROSE VILLA. to convey the gun tackle of No.4 Section

No.4 Section will proceed to Wagon lines independently on completion of relief.

Each limber driver will know what Section he is detailed as transport for.

When relieved, gun teams of Nos.1 & 3 Sections will bring their guns tackle etc to Coy. H.Q. and load them on the limber that has been detailed for them.

Section Sergeants will report to Coy. H.Q. when the loading is complete.

In the event of hostile shelling the limbers of 127 M.G. Coy. proceeding to ROSE VILLA will off load at Coy. H.Q.. If it is not possible for limber to go to Coy.H.Q. their respective guides will stop them at the "T" Cross Roads and they will off load there.

Appendix E.

      Similarly under such circumstances the guides will stop 125 M.G.Coy. limbers at the "T" Cross Roads or at Coy.H.Q. and gun teams will have to carry gun tackle to Coy. H.Q. or the "T" Cross Roads as the case may be.

---

5. REPORTS.   Officers Commanding Sections will report Relief Complete to Coy. H.Q. personally or in writing by the code word K.O.K.

Appendix F.

To 125th Infantry Brigade.

(a) Tactical lessons learnt during the month.

1. The necessity of splinter proof headcover for machine gun emplacements.

2. The advantage of properly constructed concrete emplacements to withstand heavy shelling in fixed positions.
In such positions there may be two guns which simplifies control and administration.

3. The gun, as a rule, should have one job only, e.g., it appears inadvisable to use a gun intended for close defence work on S.O.S. lines. Guns employed on barrage or harassing fire can better perform these duties.

(b) Technical lessons learnt.

1. Long field mountings.
These should be employed in all covered in emplacements to reduce the size of loopholes to a minimum. They are also very satisfactory to leave in fixed positions where guns are used for indirect overhead fire, as they give a firm platform which does not shift.

2. Aeroplane Mounting.
The new girder type of aeroplane mounting issued to the Company for trial with arm supporting ammunition box has proved very satisfactory. The only drawback is that owing to the height of the gun from the coverhead, there is considerable vibration which is communicated to the ammunition box, and unless No. 2 keeps a firm hold upon the latter, number 3 stoppages are very likely to occur.

3. This Company has found the latest type of J.H. Stewards' luminous Clinometer invaluable. It is small enough to rest on the front cover, extremely portable and does not get out of adjutsment easily.

4. All concrete emplacements should be built with a ventilating shaft. This seldom seems to be the case.

G.K. 30
20/10/17

Copy. War Diary   Appendix G.

                                                          M.G.1.
SECRET.

125th Brigade.

Reference 15th Corps No. 51/10/ G, forwarded to us
by you for suggestions.

1. The following points seem worthy of consideration:-
   The Company of eight guns definitely attached to a Brigade
   does not appear any more suitable than the present Company of
   sixteen, since it would involve the same amount of routine
   and other work with a greatly diminished staff, and the
   eight guns would be subjected to precisely the same conditions,
   tactical and otherwise, as the sixteen are at the present time.

2. It is suggested that taking all things into consideration
   it is unfair both to Infantry Commanders and to the Machine
   Guns concerned to attach these guns to Officers who have neither
   tactical or technical experience in the use of the weapon.
   It is submitted that the contention that machine gun fire is a
   concentrated and intensified form of rifle fire and that the
   ballistics of the machine gun are similar to those of the rifle
   is misleading owing to the fact that the machine gun has as
   its most essential part a fixed platform and that therefore
   indirect and barrage fire is made possible.
   It appears therefore, and experience has proved that,
   since Infantry Officers cannot be expected to devote their
   time to the specialised training necessary to the employment
   of machine guns in these spheres of action (and it is argued that
   the role played by "going over guns" might be and often is
   played equally well by the infantry weapon, the Lewis Gun) it
   would be well to dissociate machine guns as far as possible from
   the infantry using them as an auxiliary arm rather than as one
   definitely controlled by Infantry Commanders.

3. To effect this it is suggested that, working on the 56
   gun basis Divisional Machine Gun Battalions might be formed,
   consisting of Headquarters, Commanded by the D.M.G.O. (Lieut-
   Colonel) with an Adjutant and a Headquarters Staff similar to
   that of an Infantry Battalion and two Sections of four guns
   each complete as a standing Divisional Reserve.
   The remaining 48 guns could be organized in three Wings of
   sixteen each or four of twelve for purposes of administration,
   in exactly the same way as the companies in an Infantry Battalion
   are now run.
   The Transport for the whole could be Commanded by a
   Captain with one Subaltern to assist him and an adequate
   supply of trained N.C.Os.
   The whole to form the Divisional Machine Gun Battalion
   and to be classed as Divisional Troops.

4. It is submitted that in this way the Divisional Commander,
   through the D.M.G.O. would have very much the same control
   over the machine guns in the Division as he has over the
   Divisional Artillery, i.e., Direct personal control through
   an Officer on his Staff. The liaison with Brigades could be
   arranged as it is at present in the R.A., an Officer being
   detailed by the D.M.G.O. for this duty with each Brigade.

5. It is claimed that this scheme would abolish one of the
   main troubles experienced in a Machine Gun Company in the
   Field, i.e., The organization of an Orderly Room with a small
   Staff; that the guns would be better co-ordinated and a great
   deal easier handled by Division in major operations; that the
   Brigade Commander and subordinate Commander would be absolved

                                                          from

Appendix G.

(2)

from the responsibility of co-ordinating the defence of their line or offensive operations with a technical weapon whose use could equally well be delegated to a Senior Officer on Divisional Staff (the D.M.G.O.) after consultation with Brigade Commanders; and that a conference of D.M.G.Os. would very possibly furnish the Corps Commander with a more detailed report on the Machine Gun defences of the Corps front than the single handed efforts of the Corps Machine Gun Officer could.

6. A skeleton establishment of such a Machine Gun Battalion drawn up as an experiment by this Unit seems to show that instead of the Personnel having to be increased there would be a slight diminution, thus freeing a small number of men at Transport for other units.

Signed
R.V. Gery.
Captain,

27. 10. 17.   Commanding, 125th Machine Gun Company.

APPENDIX. H.

STATEMENT SHOWING STRENGTH OF COMPANY, CASUALTIES ETC.

	Off.	O.R.
Strength of Company October 1st 1917. (Including 2 Officers and 15 O.R.)	11	213.
Drafts. etc.		5.
		218.

CASUALTIES.	Offs.	O.R.
Killed.	–	–
Died of Wounds	–	–
Wounded	–	1.
Wounded (Gas)	–	–
Wounded & Missing	–	1.
Hospital		7.
		8.

	Off.	O.R.
Strength on Nov.1st.1917 (Including 2 Off. & 15 O.R.)	11	210.

	Off.	O.R.
Number in Field Ambulance during month of Oct.	1.	11
" rejoined from Field Ambulance		4
" proceeded on leave during month		11
" rejoined from leave during month	1	5
" proceeded on Duty to U.K.		3
	2.	34.

HORSES ETC. IN POSSESSION.

On Oct.1st. 1917	Officers Chargers.	Horses L.D.	Mules.
	7.	37	12

Evacuated during month
Killed   2 horses
Wounded   –
Sick   –
Cast   2 horses
Divisional Wing 1 Horse

		5	
	7	32	12
Animals drawn during month			3
Present Strength	7	32	15

Confidential

WAR DIARY.

for.
125 Machine Gun Company.
from
November 1st 1917 to November 30th 1917.

VOLUME XI

Army Form C. 2118

WAR DIARY
or
INTELLIGENCE SUMMARY
(Erase heading not required.)

125 COMPANY,
M.G.C.

NOVEMBER 1917.

Place	Date 1917.	Hour	Summary of Events and Information	Remarks and references to Appendices
BELGIUM FRANCE FURNES 1/40000 W18d53.	Nov. 1.	8:30 a.m. 12:30 2.0-3.0 p.m.	Physical Training. Section Inspection. Elementary Drills. Close Order Drill. Gas Drill. Immediate action. Aeroplane Drill.	WC.
	Nov. 2.	9 a.m.-12:30 2.0-4.0 p.m.	Route March, Company less Transport. Route AUSTRALIA CAMP – COXYDE – COXYDE BAINS – LA PANNE BAINS – LAPANNE – KERKEPANNE – AUSTRALIA CAMP. Distance 8 miles. Filling Sand Bags & Sand Bagging Instn.	WC.
	Nov. 3.	8:15 12:30	Physical Training. Sand Bagging Instn. Company Inspection. Inspection of guns & Limbers packed.	WC. WC.
	Nov. 4.		Church Parade.	
	Nov. 5.	8:30 a.m. 12:0. 2:05-4:0	Physical Training. Sand Bagging Instn. Immediate action. Immediate action. Sand Bagging Instn. 2/Lt. W.A. HARRISON rejoined from C.R.S.	WC.
125. NIEUPORT NIEUPORT.	Nov. 6.	9:0-12:15 2:0-4:0	Section at disposal of Section Officer. Officers & personnel for going up the line. Battery Parade. LIEUT. M.A.S. BREDFORD proceeded on 14 days leave to U.K.	WC.
	Nov. 7.	8:30 a.m. 12:15 3:30 p.m.	Physical Training. Preparation for relief. Sections 1, 3 & 4 Sections relieved 3 Sections of 127 Machine Gun Company in the NIEUPORT Sector with 12 guns. Relief complete 8.45 p.m. 2/LIEUT. W.N. STRAWSON to Gas Course. LIEUT. A.L. HERRIDGE proceeded to Vickers Course CAMIERS.	Appendix A. Relief Orders. WC.
	Nov. 8.		Weather: Heavy ground & wind, good visibility.	Enemy Artillery moderately active. WC.
	Nov. 9.		Dull. Wind fair visibility.	Our machine gun at M28c2350 fired 750 rounds harassing fire during the night on Road Junction at M17c1557 & Army School FLIXECOURT. Capt. H.B. CARLISLE proceeded on a Course to 4th Army School FLIXECOURT. WC.

1875 Wt. W593/826 1,000,000 4/15 J.B.C. & A. A.D.S.S./Forms/C. 2118.

Army Form C. 2118

WAR DIARY
or
INTELLIGENCE SUMMARY
(Erase heading not required.)

125 COMPANY.
M.G.C.
NOVEMBER 1917.

Instructions regarding War Diaries and Intelligence Summaries are contained in F.S. Regs., Part II. and the Staff Manual respectively. Title Pages will be prepared in manuscript.

Place	Date 1917	Hour	Weather	Summary of Events and Information	Remarks and references to Appendices
BELGIUM / FRANCE	Nov 5-10 1/10000		Squally wind. SW. Fair visibility.	One machine gun at M26c2350 fired 1000 rounds on crops trench at M17c7292. Ground emplacement at M28d6570 (Y5-) damaged by direct hit (S.7.) 1 O.R. wounded.	WM
NIEUPORT	Nov 11		Dull, some rain. Wind light W. Fair visibility.	Our machine guns kept laid on S.O.S. lines not employed for harassing fire. F4 gun team relieved. Capt G.C. KAY assumed command of Company. LIEUT. E.E. WARD appointed second in command.	WM
	Nov 12		Fine, hazy, no wind, poor visibility.	LIEUT. H.A. SALE rejoined Company from XV Corps School.	WM
	Nov 13		Fine, light wind E. Fair visibility	Y6 team relieved Y8 emplacement at M28&58C3 blown in about 4.30 a.m. 2 O.R. buried + dugout wounded. 2 Guns moved M21 d 1052. Team relieved. Aerial artillery activity. Enemy used gas shells from 9.0 p.m. to 9.30 p.m. night. CAPT. A.V. GERY R.C. M.D.S. LIEUT. E.E. WARD #10.R reported to Coy H.B. LIEUT. H.A. SALE reported to Coy H.B. and relieved 2nd Lieut. W.A. HARRISON. 2nd LIEUT. W.N. STRAWSON & 2.O.R. returned from 42 Div. Gas School. 1 O.R. to Field Ambulance.	WM
	Nov 14			Y13 & Y13a guns damaged by shell fire. Two reserve guns from transport lines replaced these. 2nd Lieut W.N. STRAWSON relieved Lieut J.A. CYMER in REDAN. LIEUT. J.A. CYMER joined Lieut. S. DICKINSON in ROSE VILLA. 1 O.R. from course.	WM
	Nov 15		Fine. Wind WSW. Light, good visibility.	1 O.R. returned from Field Ambulance. 3 O.R. to Field Ambulance (2 wounded-gas).	WM

1875 Wt. W593/826 1,000,000 4/15 J.B.C. & A. A.D.S.S./Forms/C. 2118.

Army Form C. 2118

WAR DIARY
INTELLIGENCE SUMMARY

125 COMPANY.
M.G.C.
NOVEMBER 1917

(Erase heading not required.)

Place	Date 1917	Hour	Weather	Summary of Events and Information	Remarks and references to Appendices
BELGIUM NIEUPORT	Nov 16		Cloudy, ground mist. Poor visibility. No wind.	1.O.R. to Field Ambulance. Lieut. C.R. GREEN H.A.L.G.H. and 1.O.R. attached from 4/1 LAN. FUS.	Nil
	Nov 17		Dull, misty. Poor visibility.	2/Lieut.	Nil
	Nov 18		Dull, W. wind. Fair visibility.	Noisy day. NIEUPORT and bridge near R.E. shelled. 4.6" position shelled with 5.9" and 9.2" impt. 1800 rounds fired on M17a 55.70. 3.O.R. on leave to U.K. quiet night.	Nil APPENDIX B. Operation Order No 8. Troops Moved
	Nov 19			1.O.R. to M.G.T.C. GRANTHAM. L/CPL. GREENWOOD. Relieved by FRENCH. Operation Order attached. Relief complete 9.30 p.m. Travelled to AUSTRALIA CAMP.	Nil
DUNKERQUE 1A 1/100000 HAZEBROUCK 1/100000	Nov 20	6.45am	Company less transport marched to BERGUES	Company less transport marched to ADINKERQUE entraining 9.45. Travelled by barge to BERGUES arriving about 2 p.m. Marched from BERGUES to WORMHOUDT 6 miles. Billetted there for night. Transport travelled direct by road via HOUTHEM, HANDSCHOOTE. LIEUT. J.A. CLYMER proceeded on leave to U.K.	Nil
	Nov 21	9.20am	Company marched from WORMHOUDT to HARDIFORT there for the night. Distance 4½ miles		Nil
	Nov 22	7.55am	Company marched from HARDIFORT to STAPLE & billetted	Company marched from HARDIFORT & cross roads 1 mile N.W. of STAPLE. there for the night. Distance 5½ miles.	Nil
	Nov 23	8.15am	Company marched from STAPLE to LE PECQUEUR & billetted there. Distance 8 miles	LIEUT. M.A.S. BREDSFORD returned from leave.	Nil

WAR DIARY or INTELLIGENCE SUMMARY

(Erase heading not required.)

Army Form C. 2118

125th COMPANY M.G.C.
NOVEMBER 1917.

Place	Date 1917	Hour	Summary of Events and Information	Remarks and references to Appendices
FRANCE Ind. Rd. HAZEBROUCK 1/10000	Nov 24	9.0 a.m. to 12.30 noon 2.30 p.m.	Sections at disposal of section Officers, cleaning guns &c. C.O's Inspection. Inspection of guns & equipment.	WK. WK.
	Nov 25	2 p.m.	Church Parades cleaning limber	WK.
	Nov 26	10 am 12.20 2.30 p.m.	Small Tactical scheme Stretcher carrying into action. Company marched to Baths at STEENBECQUE. I/c Maj. g. Limber. 2/Lieut. W.A. HARRISON & Infantry Course XI Corps School	WK.
	Nov 27	7.55 a.m.	Company marched from LE PECQUEUR to road crossing canal at HAZEBROUCK 6H 84 5P. Billetted for the night. Capt. G.C. KAY & Lieut. H.A. SALE proceeded to reconnoitre.	WK.
	Nov 28	9.30 a.m. to 12.30 2.0 & 4.0	Packing & cleaning limbers, overhauling gun Table Re Ests., 1 pack gun sent in advance into gun positions to be relieved.	WK.
HESDIGNEUL Central Ontario Map 1/4 0000	Nov 29	4.0 a.m. 7 a.m.	Company marched to new Company H.Q. at LE PREOL F15 C 6050. Via ESSARS - LE QUESNOY, distance 4½ miles. The company relieved 16 guns of the 73rd machine Gun Co. & with 16 guns in the LA BASSEE CANAL sector. Relief complete 11.30 a.m. Operation Orders attached.	Appendix C. Operation Orders. Appendix D Monthly Return. WK.
	Nov 30		1 O.R. & 3 horses killed by a stray shell at Thorollety strength state appended.	WK. Maj. & Capt. P.A. 125 Infr. Cav. 2 125 Infr. 1/12/17.

APPENDIX A.

SECRET   Copy No. 2

RELIEF ORDERS
by
CAPTAIN R V GERY,
COMMANDING " RAIN "
─────────────────

In the Field.   6th November, 1917.

1. RELIEF.   RAIN will relieve RUT in the Brigade Sector with
12 guns on the evening 7th November.

   Relief will commence (from C.H.Q. NIEUPORT) at 5-30 pm
7th November.

   "Relief Complete" will be reported to C.H.Q. as above
by code word "BESS".

2. DETAIL.   The following sections will relieve

   No. 1 Section (2/Lt. S. Dickinson) relieves No. 4 Section
   RUT (H.Q. ROSE VILLA).

   No. 3 Section (less one gun) (2/Lt. W.A. Harrison)
   relieves No. 1 Section RUT (H.Q. 5 Brdiges.)

   No. 4 Section (plus one gun of No. 3 Section) (Lieut Clymer)
   relieves No. 3 Section RUT (H.Q. REDAN.).

   Teams as follows :-

         No. 1 Section................4 per gun
         No. 3 Section................5 per gun
         No. 4 Section................5 per gun

   Section H.Q. as usual.
   Company H.Q. as detailed by Captain Kay.

3. PARADE:- Sections will parade as follows with limbers as shewn :-

         "A"   No. 1   3-30 pm   1 Limber   4 guns
         "B"   No. 3   4-0 pm   1 Limber   4 guns
         "C"   No. 4   4-30 pm   1 Limber   4 guns
         "D"   H.Q.   5-30 pm.   1 Limber.   -

   Guides will meet at PELICAN BRIDGE as under :-

         "A"   5-30 pm
         "B"   6-0 "
         "C"   6-30 "
         "D"   7-30 "

   "A" will proceed direct to ROSE VILLA

   "B")
   "C") To Company H.Q.   NIEUPORT.
   "D")

4. KIT AND EQUIPMENT:-

   The following kit and equipment will be taken in :-

         Guns Complete
         Tripods Mark IV.
   One belt filling machine per section otherwise all usual
   accessories less Hyposcopes, belt boxes and spare parts boxes.

(2)

Belt boxes, petrol tins, Longfield Trench Mountings and
other trench stores, (including Bulk S.A.A.) will be taken
over and receipts exchanged. These to be at C.H.Q. by
~~8th~~ November.
12 noon 8th.

Greatcoats will be taken in under section arrangements.

5. REPORT:- Following Reports to be rendered to C.H.Q. :-

    Situation Report - ("situation unchanged" will not
                              be rendered).

    Intelligence - (As per attached pro forma)

    Strength Return by Teams & H.Q. - by 6 pm daily.

    Casualty Return - As necessary

                                          Captain,
                        Commanding, 125th M.G. Coy.

Issued at 9 pm.

    Copies to :-

      1   War Diary
      2   File
3-5   Sections (1, 3, 4)
      ~~9 ADT~~
6   ~~8~~ T.O.
    ~~10.~~ Captain Kay
    ~~11~~

Appendix 13.   COPY NO: W.D

OPERATION ORDER NO: 6.
by Capt. G. L. Kay.
Commanding 125th M.G. Company.

18-11-17.

1. The Vickers Guns of 125 M.G. Coy. will be relieved 19/20th November as under:—

No. of Gun.	Relieving Unit	H. Qrs.
Y.4, Y.6, Y.7, Y.7.A.	5/321 Inf. Regt.	Right Battn. RUBBER HOUSE.
Y.5	102 Chasseur Regt.	SARDINERIE.
Y.7.B	6/321 Infy. Regt.	{ Left Battn. RUBBER House.
Y.8, Y.8.A, Y.9.A, Y.9.B, Y.9, Y.10, Y.13, Y.13.A	116 Chasseur Regt	{ Reserve Battn. NEW PARADE.

2. OC. "A" Group will send 2 guides from Y.4. and 2 guides from Y.6. to be at T. cross Roads (at this end (ZOUAVE TRACK)) at 5-30 P.M. 19th inst. to guide limbers of 5/321 Regt. to Coy. H.Q. where they will unload. They will then conduct the teams to their respective positions. Time and place at which guides are required for Y.5. to be notified later.

OC. B. Group will send 3 guides from Y.7.& Y.7.A. to be at T. cross roads at 6.P.M. 19th inst. to guide limbers of 5/321 Regt. to Coy. HQ. where they will unload. They will then conduct the team to their respective positions. Time & place at which guides are required for Y.7.B. to be notified later.

OC. C. Group will make his own arrangements with OC. 116 Chasseur Regt.

(Cont'd)

(Sheet 2.) Contd.

Limbers will be sent up as follows:-
 Coy. H.Qs. 1 limber at 5-30 p.m. at Coy. H.Q.
 A. GROUP. 2 " " 8-30 p.m. at " "
 B. GROUP. 2 " " 9. 0 p.m. at " "
 C. GROUP. 3 " " (time to be notified), at Rose Villa.

Horses for Officers will be arranged if possible.
Sections will move off independently as soon as relief is complete under Section Officers.

<u>4.</u> "Relief Complete" will be reported personally by O.s.C. A. & B. GROUPS., & by runner by O.C. C. GROUP.

<u>5.</u> Sections will proceed by Pelican Bridge - Oost. DUNKERQUE to AUSTRALIA CAMP.

<u>6.</u> Breakfasts 20th inst. 5-30 A.M.

<u>7.</u> Company will parade less Transport, ready to move off at 6.30 A.M. 20th inst.:- DRESS. Marching Order; water bottle filled. The unexpended portion of the days ration will be carried.
 Order of March:-
  Headquarters
  No. 1 SECTION.
   " 2 "
   " 3 "
   " 4 "

Packs will be carried unless otherwise ordered.

<u>8.</u> Section Officers will see that limbers are left completely and properly packed when the parade falls in.

<u>9.</u> Officers are allotted to Sections as follows:- after relief.
 No. 1 Section 2/Lt. S. Aitchison.
 " 2. Lt. J.A. Clymer.
 " 3. 2/Lt. C.R. Greenhalgh.
  Lt. H.A. Sale.
 " 4. 2/Lt. W.N. Strawson.

<u>10.</u> All Headquarters baggage will be ready to be loaded at 5-30 p.m. 19th inst. Headquarters under Sgt. Greenwood will accompany limber except:-
   3 Signallers.
   3 Runners.

Sheet 3.) contd

11. Instructions re. receipts for French Stores as already issued will be carried out.

12. 4 Other ranks will report to OC. B. Group at 5.30 P.m. 10th inst and 4 other ranks to OC A. Group, at the same time.

13. All defence schemes, trench maps, aeroplane photographs and details of work on hand or projected will be handed over on relief. Maps useful for move to be kept.

14. All dug outs and gun emplacements will be handed over in a clean and sanitary condition and a certificate rendered by O.s.C. Sections that this has been done. All rubbish will be burned.
   Sergt. Greenwood is responsible for Coy. H.Q. in this respect.

15. O.s C. Sections and Sergt Greenwood for H.Q. are responsible that quarters at AUSTRALIA CAMP are handed over in a clean and sanitary condition. Certificates to this effect will be rendered.

16. Any blankets still in use will be returned to C.Q.M.S. by ration limbers tonight.

17. PUTNEY BRIDGE will be used for in traffic.
   CROWDER for out.

18. ACKNOWLEDGE.

Issued at 6. P.m. by Orderly.

No. 1. File
    2. OC A. Group
    3. " B "
    4. " C "
    5. Rear H.Q. "
    6. Bde. H.Q. "

(Signd) G. L. Kay.
Captain
Commanding 125th M.G. Coy.

Appendix B.

Copy No. W. Diary

ADMINISTRATIVE ORDER TO ACCOMPANY

OPERATION ORDER No 6.

13-11-17.

1. Transport Officer will detail limbers on 19th inst as laid down in operation Order No 6.

2. Riding horses as arranged verbally.

3. Transport of 125th M.G.Coy and 125th L.T.M.B. will move from CANADA CAMP to WORMHOUDT "A" Area under order of T.O. 125th M.G. Coy. by road F2.c.06 - Road F76 - BRIDGE E12D 5.7 BULSCAMP - ZWAENTJE - HOLLTHEM - HANDSCHOOTE.
Transport to be South of LA PANNE - COXYDE VILLE ROAD by 8 a.m. 20th inst.
    Not to enter FERNES under any condition.
Transport will parade ready to move off at 6-40 a.m. 20th inst. Unexpended portion of the day's ration will be carried.

4. On the march units will maintain a distance of 200 yds. between Companies and transport of equivalent road space. Times have been calculated for this so units will not halt should they find they have lessened the distance.

5. Baggage Wagons and the G.S Wagons allowed for the move will march with 1st Line Transport of the unit to which they are allotted.

6. 2 G.S Wagons (1 for M.G.Coy. and 1 for L.T.M.Bs.) will be met by representatives from Units at AUSTRALIA CAMP at 3.p.m. Particulars will be obtained from D.T.O.

7. Supplies.
    T.M.B. and M.G. Coy. will draw supplies from Supply Officer, Divisional Troops on 18th inst (adjoining present place) and from Supply Officer 125th Brigade on

/contd.

2

20th at WORMHOUDT (in square)

   (a) Rations will be drawn by 1st Line Transport or lorry if preferred.

   (b) C.Q.M.S. will enquire from Supply Officer as to next days refilling point if already not notified by Brigade.

   (c) Units will draw immediately on arrival in new areas.

8. The C.Q.M.S. will arrange for Hot Water on arrival of Company at WORMHOUDT "A" area.

9. Leave.— Officers and other ranks proceeding on leave will depart from Railhead. Orders re leave parties will be complied with as far as possible.

   Nov. 19. LEFFRINCKHOUCKE
        21. ARNEKE
        22.)
        23.) EBBLINGHEM

10. T.O. and Section Officers will see that all quarters and lines at AUSTRALIA CAMP and elsewhere on the move are left clean. Certificates will always be rendered to this effect prior to departure.

11. 2/Lt W.A. HARRISON and the Q.M.S. will proceed with bicycles to the WORMHOUDT A. Area with billeting certificate and lists of distribution (which will be sent down 19th inst.) Billeting Certificates will be handed to Area Commandants.

   This party together with T.M.D. billeting Party will depart in time to report to Staff Captain at 9 a.m. 20th inst. at Area Commandant's Office WORMHOUDT A. Area.

One of this party will meet units to guide them to billets.

M.G Coy and T.M.B. will arrive at BERGUES by barge during afternoon of 20th

12. Section Officers will detail 2 men per Section as brakesmen to report to T.O. at 6.30 am. There will **not** be more than one brakesman per limber. Surplus details will march with H.QRS

13. ACKNOWLEDGE

(signed) G.C Ray. Captain
Commanding 125th M.G. Company.

Issued at 4.30pm. by orderly.

Copy No 1 File.
2 CQMS
3
4
5 } Section Officers.
6

M.G. Form "C."

INTER-MACHINE GUN COMPANY RELIEF.

This Form will be handed over to the Relieving Machine Gun Company Commander and a copy given to the Relieving Brigade.

125 M.G. Coy. to .... M.G. Coy. Date 16/4/17 1917.

No. of Gun.	Gun Map Location.	Map Location of Target.	NIGHT LINE OF FIRE.			Ammunition at gun position, per gun.		Remarks.
			Range to Target.	Quadrant Elevation in Minutes.	C.R.Q. Compass Bearing.	Belt Boxes.	S.A.A. Boxes.	
1	2	3	4	5	6	7		8
Y.9.a.	M.28.a.0305.	M.24.d.2948. LONK TRACK	1600x	161x	31° 30'			
Y.9.B.	M.28.a.0505.	M.28.b.5300.	1600x	161'	32°			
Y.9.	M.27.b.9527.	M.28.3842. LONK TRACK	1500x	142'	31° 30'			
Y.10.	M.27.b.9527.	M.28.2274. to	1500x	142'	31° 30'			
Y.8.	M.21.D.1052.	Close defence guns			110°			
Y.8.a.	do.				116°			
Y.13.	M.21.d.7510.	M.28.d.7040.1800x-2000x 260'-246'			84°			
Y.13.a.	M.21.d.7536.	M.28.0945. 2000x-2900x 260'-320'			89°			

Group 6

Map location of Section Officer or depôt for Guns Nos. Y.9. A. to Y.13.A. at M.27.6. Ny 10. with .... boxes S.A.A. and .... belts.
" " Remaining Guns: No. .... " " Nos. .... No. .... at .... with .... boxes S.A.A. and .... belts.
" " " " No. .... at .... with .... boxes S.A.A. and .... belts.
" " Company Headquarters .... No. .... at .... with .... boxes S.A.A. and .... belts.
Brigade Headquarters at ....

NOTES:—1.—M.G. defence scheme shewing all gun positions with lines of fire will be handed over, together with indirect fire schemes and plans for improvement of works, etc.

2.—At each gun position, the information relating to the gun in position will be entered on the Sentry Order Board or Range Card. Map location of Company and Brigade Headquarters will NOT be posted at the Machine Gun position.

Name ....

Rank .... Captain ....

Commanding .... 125 .... M.G. Company.

4th Field Survey Coy., R.E. 1629 26-7-17

M.G. Form "C."

This Form will be handed over to the Relieving Machine Gun Company Commander and a copy given to the Relieving Brigade.

............125............M.G. Coy. to............M.G. Coy. Date......16/11/17......1917.

INTER-MACHINE GUN COMPANY RELIEF.

No. of Gun.	Gun Map Location.	NIGHT LINE OF FIRE.				Ammunition at gun position, per gun.		Remarks.
		Map Location of Target.	Range to Target.	Quadrant Elevation in Minutes.	Compass Bearing.	Belt Boxes.	S.A.A. Boxes.	
1	2	3	4	5	6	7		8
					6010			
A {	1.4.M.2a.76	} Front defence guns.			245°–12°			
Group {	2.3 Lithery M.2.gc 5265				299°–213°			
	Y.C.N.26d 6570				238°–277°			
Y {	Y.7.M.25a.4930	} Most lifting guns.			29°–60°			
B {	Y.7. "				301°–340°			
Group {	Y.7.M.25a.936				295°–334°			

Map location of Section Officer or depôt for Guns Nos. 4.5.1.6. at M.2gc. 1660. with .... boxes S.A.A. and .... belts.
" " Remaining Guns: No. .... Nos. .... at .... with .... boxes S.A.A. and .... belts.
" " " " No. M.2&C.7525. at .... with .... boxes S.A.A. and .... belts.
" " Company Headquarters at .... Brigade Headquarters at .... with .... boxes S.A.A. and .... belts.

NOTES:—1.—M.G. defence scheme shewing all gun positions with lines of fire will be handed over, together with indirect fire schemes and plans for improvement of works, etc.

2.—At each gun position, the information relating to the gun in position will be entered on the Sentry Order Board or Range Card. Map location of Company and Brigade Headquarters will NOT be posted at the Machine Gun position.

Name............ Rank......Captain............

Commanding......125......M.G. Company.

4th Field Survey Coy., R.E. 1620 26-7-17

Appendix B.

SECRET   Appendix C.   Copy No. 7

125th Machine Gun Company.

Order No. 8.

By

Captain G. C. Kay.

In The Field
28/11/17.

REF. MAP. 1/40000.
BETHUNE
1/10000. 36° N.W.I
1/20.000. 36° S.E.
1/20.000. 36° N.E.

1. The 125th Machine Gun Coy. will relieve the 75th Machine Gun Coy. on the 29th inst.

2. Relief will commence at 7. A.M. at Coy. H.Q. F.15. B.60.50. Pack animals will be used, as per attached time table.

3. Signalling Corporal will detail 1 signaller to accompany relief to each group. H.Q. and return to Coy. H.Q. on relief complete.

4. Relief complete will be reported in writing by the code word TWERP. by the signaller returning.

5. ACKNOWLEDGE.

Issued At.   By Orderly.

No. 1. File
    2. O.C. 75th M.G. Coy.
    3. A. Group.
    4. B. Group.
    5. C. Group.
    6. T. O.
    7. War Diary
    8. 2nd in Command.

Captain
Commanding
125 M.G. Coy.

Relief tables: Issued with 135" M.G. by. to Order No."

SERIAL NO.	DATE	SECTION	FROM	TO	RELIEVING	REMARKS
A.Coy.?	2/5	No.1 - 2 guns (Cool.) S&b (N.C.O. & 10 men)	P15.C.6050.	A.25.D.82 central (Mandatory) at gun position	Nov.15. Section of Barrage Pl. of C. Coy.	Relief to be complete by 7am. S.H.Q. C.Coy.23.
B.Coy.?	"	M.3 + 1 gun. (No. 2 -7 - Teams)	do.	Junction of Mont. SY & Kenava SY. A.14.D. 3510. Handy Lane D.	5 guns Munitaah SI.T.H.G.T.E.	Relief to be complete by noon. S.H.Q. Gunn.Pedan. A.14.4412
C.Coy.?	"	No 4 gun / 1 gun (No. 2 - 8 - Teams)	do.	do.	5 guns. Munitaah area	Relief to be complete by noon. S.H.Q. Gun.View
					V.50.A.15.2 A.15.52.A.M.' A.M. C. links.	

Note.

1. Guides of the 75th. M.G.Bn. will meet gun teams at Bn H.Q.

2. Ammunition boxes & belts will be taken over. 12 per gun Barrage guns. 8 per gun remainder.

3. Petrol cans will be taken over at gun position.

4. A group will not take tripods but will take 5 Snowker Boards and 1 Aux. Mounting.

SECRET   Copy No 3

Administrative Orders
By
Captain E. C. Kay
Commanding 125th M.G. Company
To accompany O. Orders. No: 8.

1. The following kits will be taken into the trenches:-
    Guns in trench bags & aux. mountings. Spare parts cases
            Condensers + Bag.
    Tripods (except as detailed for A. group)
    2 Spare parts boxes per group at S.H.Q.

2. No. 1 section will hand over 1 tripod complete to No. 3
    section and obtain a receipt for same.

3. DRESS:- Fighting Order. Greatcoats will be carried.

4. RATIONS & WATER. Section Officers will ascertain water
            points:- The water supply is good.
    Rations will be sent up each evening at a time
            to be notified later.
    Teams will take the unexpended portion and 1
    days ration in with them on the 29th inst.

5. The following reports will be rendered daily by 6. A.M.
    prompt:- Intelligence reports, as per pro-forma
    issued herewith.
            Casualty Return.
            Ammunition expended.
            Sick Report.
            Ration Strength by teams.
    Situation reports will be rendered if & when
        any unusual occurrence takes place.

6. Harassing fire will be carried on as by 75th
    M.G. Coy. till further orders.
                                        (Contd)

(Continued).   2

6. Targets & calculations will be submitted to Bay. H.Q. daily as per attached pro-formas for the following night by 6.A.M. runner.

7. Defense schemes, aeroplane photographs and sketches will be taken over on relief. A list in DUPLICATE of these & all trench stores will be rendered to Bay. H.Q. by 6. A.M. 30th inst.

8. Allindents for R.E. material will be submitted by 6.A.M. daily 2 days in advance in the following form:—
   Group requiring material.
   Material required. Quantity. Date.
   Place of delivery.
   For what required.
   (In cases of camouflage, nature of surroundings required.)

9. Section officers will get into touch with Sections on their Right and Left, and will also report to the Battalion Commander of their Sector as soon as possible after relief, and get into touch with the nearest Company Commander.

10. Locations as per separate list
   Location
   Gum Boot Stores.
   Left Battalion. PONT FIXÉ (A14c central) NR. GUINCHY STATION.
   Right Battalion. ROAD JUNCTION (A20b3.1.)
   Divisional Soup Kitchen & Canteen. ROAD JUNCTION (A20 b 3.1.) Free soup.

   RE DUMPS.
   (a) Corps RE Dump – BEUVRY.
   (b) PONT FIXÉ (Bde). A14 a 20.
   (c) ROAD JUNCTION. A 20. b. 3. 2.

Sheet 3

10. (A) Brigade Ammunition Dump.
        PONT FIXE.
    (B) Junction Harley & Hertford St. (A.20.D.27).

    Medical.
    (A) Regimental aid Posts. PONT FIXE. (A.14.B.21.)
                              HERTFORD ST. (A.21.A.57.)
                              ROBERTSONS ALLEY. (A.27.A.69).
    (B) Bearer Relay Post. (A.14.A.98)
    (C) Advanced Dressing Station.
              LONE FARM. (A.7.D.18.).
              HARLEY ST. (A.20.D.49).

    Salvage.   Brigade Dump. F.8 B.58.
               Main Dump. LOCON.

11. The usual precautions will be taken against Trench feet. The men being told off in pairs for rubbing. Camphor powder etc will be obtained as soon as possible and supplied for sections. The usual certificate will be rendered by C.A.M. daily.

12. TRENCH DISCIPLINE.
              Men should be doing one of 3 things:-
              A. Sentry.
              B. Working.
              C. Sleeping.

    Men will be washed and shaved by 9. A.M. daily, guns arms and ammunition will be inspected daily under section arrangements.
    Rubbish will be burned or buried.
    Latrines will be kept scrupulously clean.
    Men are not allowed to wander about without equipment.
    Box respirators will always be worn at the alert.

                                              (contd).

Sheet 4 (contd).

18. Suggestions as to regrouping of B + C. groups if necessary may be submitted by group commanders.

Captain
Commanding 125 M.G. Coy.

1. Title
2. Wardiary
3.
4. O.C. A. Group.
5. — B. —
6. — C. —
7. T.O
8. 2nd in Command.
9. C.S.M.
10. C.Q.M. Sgt.

Appendix D.

Statement showing Strength of Company, casualties etc.

	OFF.	O.R.
Strength of Company on November 1st 1917. (Including 2 OFF and 15. O.R.)	11.	210.
Drafts etc. Attached for duty.	1.	2.
	12.	212.

Casualties.	OFF.	O.R.
Killed	–	–
Died of Wounds.	–	1
Wounded	–	3.
Wounded Gas.	–	3.
Wounded and missing	–	–
Hospital.	–	11
		18.

		18
Strength of Company on Dec. 1st 1917 (Including 1. off 16 O.R.).	12.	194

	OFF.	O.R.
Number in Field Ambulance during month of November.		17
" rejoined from Field Ambulance.	1.	4.
" proceeded on leave during month.	2.	17.
" rejoined from leave.	1.	15.
" proceeding on Duty to U.K.		1.
	4.	54.

Horses etc in possession

	Officers Chargers	Horses L.D.	Mules.
On Nov. 1st. 1917.	7.	32.	15.

Evacuated During Month.

Killed. 3. Officers Chargers.
Wounded –
Cast. 3 Light Draft.
Divisional Wing. 1.

	Chargers	Horses L.D.	Mules
	3.	4.	
	4.	28.	15
Drawn during month.		3.	
Present Strength.	4.	31.	15.

Vol. 11

Confidential

War Diary,
for
125th Machine Gun Company,
from
December 1st. to December 31st.
1917.

Volume XII

Army Form C. 2118

WAR DIARY
or
INTELLIGENCE SUMMARY
(Erase heading not required.)

125 Company
M.G.C.
December 1917.

Place	Date 1917.	Hour	Weather	Summary of Events and Information	Remarks and references to Appendices
FRANCE. Inf. Bgd. LA BASSEE 36c NW.1. 1/10000	Dec 1.		Dull wind S.W. mild. Visibility poor.	2 machine guns fired 3200 rounds during night on the following targets A17c4076, Cross Roads A28d45, A22c3505, A28a32 & A22c3505.	Appx.
	Dec 2		Fine wind S. mild stormy Visibility poor.	2 machine guns fired 1500 rounds on A11a5652 and A22 & 6545 during the night.	Appx.
	Dec 3		Fine wind S.W. mild Visibility good.	2 machine guns fired during night on A22 d 4363 and A11 a 0078. 2000 rounds.	Appx.
	Dec 4		Fine wind mild Visibility poor.	Usual night firing. 2000 rounds on A23c2558, A28b8595. Lt. E.E. WARD proceeded to 226 M.G. Coy. to assume command.	Appx.
	Dec 5		Fine wind S. Visibility good.	2 machine guns fired 3000 rounds during the night A17 S018, A17c0813 & A29 & 4245.	Appx.
	Dec 6		Fine wind S.W. slight Good visibility	2 machine guns fired 2500 rounds on A23c2558, A28c8595 during the night. LIEUT. J.A. HERRIDGE proceeded to U.K. on leave. LT. J.A. CLYMER rejoined from leave.	Appx.
	Dec 7		Cloudy wet, wind S.W. mild poor visibility	2 machine guns fired 4400 rounds during night at A10d9576 A11c 2593 T. A17d52. At 6 P.M. 1 gun fired 250 rounds on enemy M.G. in CANAL Bank A16c Central. CAPT. M.B. CARLISLE appointed second in command vice Lt. E.E. WARD.	Appx.
	Dec 8		Cloudy showers Wind S.W mild Visibility variable.	2 machine guns fired 3500 rounds during night on A10a78 & G5a46.	Appx.
	Dec 9		Cloudy showery Wind S.W. Visibility poor.	3 machine guns fired 5500 rounds during the night on A23 & 18, A97c3575 TA11c5652.	Appx.

1875 Wt. W593/826 1,000,000 4/15 J.B.C. & A. A.D.S.S./Forms/C. 2118.

WAR DIARY
or
INTELLIGENCE SUMMARY.
(Erase heading not required.)

Army Form C. 2118.

125 Company.
M.G.C.
December 1917.

Instructions regarding War Diaries and Intelligence Summaries are contained in F. S. Regs., Part II. and the Staff Manual respectively. Title pages will be prepared in manuscript.

Place	Date 1917	Hour	Summary of Events and Information	Remarks and references to Appendices
FRANCE				
Map Ref 36c N.W.W.	Dec. 10.		3 guns fired 3000 rounds on A.23.d.3.0 A.27.b.0.8. A.16.b.40.77. Weather fair. Wind mild S.W. Visibility fair.	MAC
LA BASSÉE 1/10,000	Dec 11.	a.m. 9.30.	125 M.G. Coy relieved in CANAL SECTOR LA BASSÉE by 16 guns 126 M.G. Coy. Relief complete at Company marched to BETHUNE & billeted at CHAMBORS BARRACKS. 125 Bde in Div Reserve	MAC
36A SE & NE 36 NW 1/40,000 BETHUNE E.27.C. 1/40,000	Dec 12.	9-12.15 a.m. 2-3.30 p.m	Inspection of kit & gun stores, cleaning etc. Kit inspection & issue of deficiencies.	MAC
	Dec 13	a.m. 9-12.30 p.m. 2.3.30	Cleaning guns, clothing, equipment. Bathing. Drill & Packing Limbers.	MAC
	Dec 14.	a.m. 9-12.15 p.m. 1.30-3.30	Inspection of Coy by C.O. Physical Training Mechanism Stripping etc. Instruction in care & handling of revolvers & range practices. Preparation of guns for range. Lecture by Section Officers DISCIPLINE.	MAC
	Dec 15	a.m 8.30.	Range practices a 300" range. Inspection of Headquarters & Transport by C.O.	MAC
	Dec 16.	a.m. 10.50.	Divine Service followed by presentation of Medal Ribbons by Divisional Commander. 125 M.G. Coy recipients Lieut R.A. SALE M.C. 39065 a/S.M. D. GREST DCM 39487 Sgt A. DIXON M.M. 39530 M.CPL C. URQU.M.M. 39302 Pte A. BROADHURST. M.M.	MAC
	Dec 17	a.m 8.30 & 2.15 2pm	Squad Drill - Gas drill. Mechanism Stripping etc. Gun Drill. & I.A. Recreational Training - Football. Lt S. DICKINSON proceeded on 4 days leave to PARIS. CAPT M.B. CATRUISE returned from 4th Army School on Assumed duties of 2nd in command	MAC

1577 Wt W10791/1773 300,000 1/15 D. D. & L. A.D.S.S./Forms/C. 2118.

Army Form C. 2118.

125 Company.
M.G.C.
December 1917.

WAR DIARY
or
INTELLIGENCE SUMMARY.
(Erase heading not required.)

Instructions regarding War Diaries and Intelligence Summaries are contained in F. S. Regs., Part II. and the Staff Manual respectively. Title pages will be prepared in manuscript.

Place	Date 1917	Hour	Summary of Events and Information	Remarks and references to Appendices
FRANCE				
Hop Ref (36a SE 36 SW) 36b NE 36 N.W.	Dec. 18.	a.m. 8.30-12 2 p.m.	Squad drill. Gas drill. I.A. Visual Training. Recreational Training - Football. LCR killed by bomb in BETHUNE	HH
BETHUNE B16 1/40000	Dec. 19	a.m. 8.30-12.15 2 p.m.	Squad drill. Gas drill. Rapid repairs & adjustments. Tactical training. Rapid coming into action - use of (gun) (to cont) Recreational training. Football - Boxing - Cross country run.	HH
36c N.W.1 1/10000 LABASSÉE 1/10000	Dec. 20	7.30-12 2 p.m.	Range practices on Boot range. Bathing. Recreational training. Boxing. Football - Lecture by Section Officers "TRENCH STANDING ORDERS" & "DUTIES OF SENTRIES."	HH
36 SW3 RICHEBOURG 1/10000	Dec. 21	a.m. 8.30-12.15 2 p.m.	Squad drill. Gas drill. Tactical training in box respirators. Lecture by T.O. "CARE OF ANIMALS". Recreational training. Boxing Football, etc. Lt A.L. HERRIDGE returned from leave to U.K. Lt H.A. SALE proceeded on leave to U.K.	HH
	Dec. 22.	a.m. 8.30-11.15	Gas drill - Preparation for the line. Lt S DICKINSON returned from leave to Paris.	HH
	Dec. 23.	a.m. 2.	125 M.G.Coy with 16 guns relieved 127 M.G Coy in the LA BASSÉE Sector Relief complete (Operation Order & Disposition map attached) (6 am) 2 guns fired 200 rounds on a target at A11a 58 55 4 A10d 95 68 Lt L SMITH proceeded on leave to U.K. 2/Lt W.A. HARRISON returned to Fy Corps School.	HH
	Dec. 24.	a.m.	Special RE Coy Discharged gas successfully & our area Selected points at 7.30 p.m. 9.40 p.m. & 11.40 p.m. - RFA: MGs & TMs co-operated. Guns fired 2400 rounds on following targets during the course of Gun Operation. A6c q8 55 A6d 43 37 A6d q4 46 A11c q3 46 A16b 32 07 A16b q2 08 A70 62 17 A11a 00	HH

WEATHER:
Clear frosty
Cold. Visibility good.

Wind null W.S.W. Thaw.

S.21c 22 36 D. D. & L.
1577 Wt. W10791/1773 500,000 1/15 A.D.S.S./Forms/C. 2118.

Army Form C. 2118.

125 Coy M.G.C.
December 1917.

WAR DIARY
or
INTELLIGENCE SUMMARY.
(Erase heading not required.)

Place	Date 1917	Hour	WEATHER	Summary of Events and Information	Remarks and references to Appendices
FRANCE Rif Map. 36c.N.W.1 LA BASSÉE 1/10000	Dec. 25		Strong N. wind decreasing later. Fair early. Snow in afternoon & evening	2 guns fired 3000 rounds on following targets A11c 10·70 & S29a 50·30.	Appx
36 S.W.3 RICHEBOURG 1/10000	Dec. 26		Strong N. wind decreasing later. Snow showers and hazy afterwards visibility bad.	3 guns fired 5000 rounds on following targets A5a 05·40 - A10a 70·80 S29b 55·40 & S28b 60·86.	Appx
	Dec. 27.		Fair. Got dull & Cloudy. Some Snow fell late.	4 guns 127 M.G. Coy. attached to 125 M.G. Coy. Took up positions at S25b10·62. S26b07·02 S26c06·09 S26c06·06 for close defence & a S.O.S battery position at S26a 0·6. (See map attached) Left Batt 1 5 guns fired 5000 rounds on following targets A5a 15·35 S29d 20·50 A9c 91·07 A11c 92·47 and A5d 30·70.	Appx
	Dec. 28.		Fine. Snowy. Wind S.E. mild. Sun fell bright. Visibility very good.	Left Battery registered. Range 2700 - OFL 2200. Clearance Satisfactory. 7 guns fired 7000 rounds on following targets S29c 70·25 - S29a 10·40 - A4c 65·35 - A4a 90·70 to A4b 39·58 - A4c 35·50 - A5c 01·61 - A11b 10·42	Appx
	Dec. 29		Fair. Dull - No Wind. Visibility poor.	New Batt position at A2a 3·7 completed. Return as 1st Batts. 2 guns left group withdraws to 1st Batts - One gun from R.F. Batts withdraws to LEPS 6 at A8a 82·82 in Village line. One gun 1st group withdraws to LEPS 3 (Village line) at A8 78·56. 3 guns fired 5000 rounds on targets at A4c 65·35 A9b 5·6. A10a 7·8. S29b 22·78 - A11c 90·44	Appx
	Dec. 30		Wind Mild. E. Dull Visibility bad.	No. 3 Sect from centre Batts relieved R group (No 4 Sect) to centre Batts. Two guns No 2 Sect from 1st Batt relieved 2 guns left group (No 1 Sect) to 1st Batts. 4 guns fired 5000 rounds on the following targets A6b 92·08, A7a 62·17 A4c 35·50 & S28b 55·40.	Appx
	Dec. 31.		Wind Mild E Dull Visibility bad.	6 guns fired 6000 rounds on the following targets S29a 53 A4c 45·38 A5a 65·36 A4c 90·81 S26c59·94 & S29a 30·75	Appx

(Attached) Appendix A S.O.S Line Operation Order No 10
Appendix B D.D. & L. Appendix C Organization in order as to
Appendix D Strength Appendix E Tactical & Technical actions learnt. Appendix F British Map

31/12/17.
[signatures]
Lieut. 125 Coy Comdg

1577 Wt. W10791/1773 500,000 1/15 D.D. & L. ADSS. (Forms/C.2118.

SECRET.   Appendix A.   Copy No. 8. W.D.

Operation Order No. 9.
by
Captain G. B. Kay.
Commanding 125th Machine Gun Company.

Ref. Maps.
1/10000. LA BASSÉE
1/20000. BÉTHUNE.

In the Field
8/12/17.

1. The 126th Machine Gun Company will relieve this Company in the line on the 11th inst.

2. Relief will commence from Company Headquarters at 9.30 a.m. 11th inst.
   Guides. One guide from each gun team of B Group and C Group will be at junction HARLEY STREET – DAWSON STREET to guide in relieving teams at 10 a.m. 11th inst.
   One guide per team from A Group will be at CHALK PIT at end of RAILWAY TRENCH to guide in relieving teams at 10 a.m. 11th inst.
   Guides from Company H.Q. will conduct reliefs to junction HARLEY STREET – DAWSON STREET and CHALK PIT respectively.

3. One half G.S. Limbered Wagon will be at junction HARLEY STREET – DAWSON STREET at 11.45 a.m. for B Group.
   One half G.S. Limbered Wagon will be at junction HARLEY STREET – DAWSON STREET at 12.15 p.m. for C Group.
   One half G.S. Limbered Wagon will be at CHALK PIT at end of RAILWAY TRENCH at 11.45 a.m. for A Group.

4. All trench stores including aeroplane photographs, maps and sketches of this area will be handed

Sheet 2.

Contd 4.
over on relief and receipts in triplicate obtained, two of which will be handed into the Orderly Room by 9 am. 12th inst.

5. Relief Complete will be reported in person by Section Officers

6. On completion of relief the Company will move into BETHUNE Barracks in E.S.C.

7. The Company will parade in column of route in front of Orderly Room, ready to move off at 1.30 pm

8. Distances on march will be:—
Company divided into two Sections 100 yards apart. Transport will march 200 yards in rear of Company.

9. ACKNOWLEDGE.

W. Henry
Captain,
O.C. 125th M.G. Company.

Issued at 9.30 am by Orderly,
Copies to: 11th Inst

Appendix A.

125 M. G. Coy.
Administrative Instructions No. 9
To accompany Operation Orders No. 9

REF. MAP. 1/10000
LA GORGUE.

In The Field
8.12.17.

1. All gun positions and dugouts will be handed over in a clean and sanitary condition and a certificate obtained to this effect and handed in to the Orderly Room by 9.0.a.m. 12th inst.

2. Fourteen boxes and fourteen belts filled per gun will be handed over and a separate receipt obtained and handed in to the Orderly Room. by 9.0.A.M. 12th inst.

3. The C.S.M. will take over 224 boxes and 224 belts, filled from 126 M. G. Coy. on 11th inst and have them dumped at the Q. M. stores as soon as possible after arrival of 126 M. G. Coy.

4. Lieut J. A. CLYMER and 2 O.R. to be detailed by C.S.M. will proceed as billeting party arriving at 126 M. G. Coy. billets by 7.30.A.M. 11th inst. They will take over all billets from 126 M. G. Coy.

5. The Orderly Sgt will see that all billets are clean by 9.30.A.M. and report to that effect to the Orderly Room. He will also see that all men at Coy. H.Q. have moved into billet no. 99 by 9.30.A.M. with the exception of the signallers on duty.

(Cont.)

(Sheet 2) Contd

6. The A.S. Wagon will be at the Q.M. Stores by 10. A.M. All Officer's Valises will be deposited there by that hour, also blankets in bundles of ten. Dinners will be at 1.0.P.M. at box N a or 4th line.

7. A motor lorry to convey baggage will arrive during forenoon of 11th inst.

The C.S.M. will detail party of men who will be unfit to march, as loading party who travel on same.

M A S Bickford Lieut.
for Captain
OC 125 M. G. Coy.

Issued at 9.30am by Orderly
9th inst.

COPIES
1. OC A Group
2. " B "
3. " C "
4. C.S.M.
5. C.Q.M. Sgt
6. M. Clynes
7. L. O.
8. W. O.
9. W. O.
10. File

Appendix A.

M.G. Form "B".

MACHINE GUN BARRAGE FIRE.

No. A. Group.   Right Barrage.   Date 10/12/17.   Map used 36.c.N.W.1. 1/10000 36.c.N.W.3. 1/10000   O.C. Group Lieut S Atkinson

Gun No. and Map Location.	Barrage Line, Map Location.	Range to Barrage Line in Yards.	ELEVATION			Q.E. in Minutes. Tables 3 (a) or 3 (b)	Range Yards Corresponding to Q.E. Table 1, Col. 2.	CLEARANCE OVER OWN TROOPS. (To be worked out for each lift).				DIRECTION.		REMARKS.		
			Contours in Yards.		V.I. in Yards.			Contour of own Troops in Yards. B.	Range to own Troops in Yards.	Traj. Height in Yards. Table 2. C.	Clearance obtained by Note (1) below.	Clearance required in Yards.	GRID Compass Bearing.	From	Firing. To	Checked by.
			Gun. A.	Barrage Line.												
	Right Barrage															
1. G.3.a.33.2	G.3.5.72	2700	95	99	2	34.8	2700	38	1650	185	182	53	101° 30'	Zero on S.O.S. going up or left hair		
2. G.3.a.34.28	G.2.8.30	2600	"	"	"	49.2	2600	"	"	158	155	"	"	Short.		
3. G.3.a.33.30	G.3.2.53	2500	"	"	"	44.3	2500	"	"	133	132	"	"	Rate of fire 250 rounds per minute for first three minutes. 25 rounds per minute		
4. G.3.a.30.34	G.3.2.09.5	2400	"	"	"	39.7	2400	"	"	113	110	"	"	for the next 20 minutes or till		
5. G.3.a.29.36	G.2.8.94	2300	"	"	"	35.5	2300	"	"	92	89	"	"	situation clears		
6. G.3.a.26.38	G.3.c.74.5	2260	"	"	"	32.0	2200	"	"	74	71	"	"			
	Left Barrage															
1. G.3.a.33.27	A.c.4.30	2700	95	27	8	54.2	2700	27	1800	184	192	60	26° 30'	Zero on S.O.S. going up Canal Centre		
2. G.3.a.34.28	A.d.3.89	2600	"	"	"	48.0	2600	"	"	155	163	"	"			
3. G.3.a.33.30	A.d.2.44	2500	"	"	"	43.7	2500	"	"	129	137	"	"	Rate of fire, the same		
4. G.3.a.30.34	A.d.1.00	2400	"	"	"	39.1	2400	"	"	105	115	"	"			
5. G.3.a.29.36	Z.d.30.a.	2300	"	"	"	34.9	2300	"	"	83	91	"	"			
6. G.3.a.26.38	Z.c.98	2200	"	"	"	30.8	2150	"	"	54	62	"	"			

NOTES.—(1) Clearance in yards equals A minus B plus or minus C according as trajectory tables give positive or negative values of C.
(2) Immediately before firing Q.E. must be corrected, if necessary, for atmospheric influences. See Table 5.
(3) For lateral wind allowance. See Table 4.
(4) If obstruction exists between gun and target, and its highest point cannot be seen, ascertain if shots will clear by substituting "obstruction" for "own troops" in clearance column above, and find clearance by rule in Note (1). Minimum clearance required equals half height of cone for range to obstruction.

4th Field Survey Coy. R.E. 1633 27-7-17   [P.T.O.

Murray Capt.
Commdy 123rd M.G. Coy

M.G. Form "B."

MACHINE GUN BARRAGE FIRE.

No. 1 B. Group. No. ..... Barrage. Date 10/12/17. Map used 36CNWI 1/10,000.

Lines 2nd Scots M.G. O.C. Group ....

		ELEVATION.					CLEARANCE OVER OWN TROOPS. (To be worked out for each lift)				DIRECTION.		REMARKS.		
Gun No. and Map Location.	Range to Barrage Line in Yards.	Contours in Yards.		V.I. in Yards.	Q.E. in Minutes. Tables 3(a) or 3(b)	Range Yards Corresponding to Q.E. Table 1, Col. 2	Contour of own Troops in Yards. B.	Range to own Troops in Yards.	Traj. Height in Yards. Table 2. C.	Clearance obtained by Note (1) below.	Clearance required in Yards.	Q.&D.	Compass Bearing.	General.	Firing.	
		Gun. A.	Barrage Line.												From To	Rounds. Checked by.
V.50. A.21.c.20.05 A.28.d.05	1750	—	—	—	189	1750	—	1000	36.	33.	20.		127°42'	Reg on ridge Sugar 150 yards this gun used for harassing fire at night at V.I. position A.21.c.035 trench 50 yds long to left of this class if enemy counter attack		
S.1. A.21.d.13 A.10.c.30	1950	—	—	—	240	1950.	—	1500.	47.	40.	40.		18°	Reid on S.O.S line used for close defence if enemy break through		
F.1. A.2.w.7:34 A.28.a.15.3	1000	—	—	—	62	—	—	Close defence.					167°			
F.2. A.2.w.19.79 A.22.c.8.50	950	—	—	—	57	—	—	Close defence					168°	In 12" pill tack there is a second emplacement facing N.		
F.3. A.22.w.18 A.11.1.03	—	—	—	—	7	—	—	Close defence					35°	In 1" pill tack there is a second emplacement facing S.		

NOTES.—(1) Clearance in yards equals A minus B plus or minus C according as trajectory tables give positive or negative values of C.
(2) Immediately before firing Q.E. must be corrected, if necessary, for atmospheric influences. See Table 5.
(3) For lateral wind allowance. See Table 4.
(4) If obstruction exists between gun and target, and its highest point cannot be seen, ascertain if shots will clear by substituting "obstruction" for "own troops" in clearance column above, and find clearance by rule in Note (1). Minimum clearance required equals half height of cone for range to obstruction.

J. Murry Capt.
Comdg 125th M.G. Coy.

4th Field Survey Coy., R.E. 1633 27-7-17   [P.T.O.

M.G. Form "B".

MACHINE GUN BARRAGE FIRE.

No. **C** Group. No. .... Barrage. Date **10/12/17**. Map used **36 C N.W.1 1/10000**. O.C. Group **269.U.T. Stevens**

Gun No. and Map Location.	Range to Barrage Line in Yards.	ELEVATION — Contours in Yards. Gun. A.	Barrage Line.	V.I. in Yards.	Q.E. in Minutes. Tables 3(a) or 3(b)	Range Yards Corresponding to Q.E. Table 1, Col. 2.	CLEARANCE OVER OWN TROOPS — Contour of own Troops in Yards. B.	Range to own Troops in Yards.	Trajy. Height in Yards. Table 2. C.	Clearance obtained by Note (1) below.	Clearance required in Yards.	DIRECTION. Grid Compass Bearing.	REMARKS — Firing From	To	Rounds.	Checked by.	General.
F4. A16c 0949 A27z 3282	350	Field of fire			95°	—	157°	Grid Bearing									Close defence. Gun not mounted by day.
A14. A1d 2838 A28 6450	2000	27	39	6	267	2050	27	950	57	5-7	18	160°					Key position S.O.S. line. Close defence if own troops through.
" A16c 0872		Field of fire			3° to 65°			Grid Bearing									Right position. Zone defence.
A15a A1d 2801 A28 6860	2000	27	22	5	248	1950	27	1100	53	33	29	8°					Raid or S.O.S. line. Close defence N.
S.2. A15a 0756 A28a 32 2230		27	33	6	351	2300	27	1500	92	92	40	164°					Raid or S.O.S. line. Close defence if enemy through or towards Guards sector.
A.14 A14 661 A36 6315	1950	27	22	5	233	1900	22	1300	38	38	40	28°					Raid or S.O.S. line. Close defence if enemy towards through or towards Guards sector.
" A14 6365		Harassing fire position.															

NOTES.—(1) Clearance in yards equals A minus B plus or minus C according as trajectory tables give positive or negative values of C.
(2) Immediately before firing Q.E. must be corrected, if necessary, for atmospheric influences. See Table 4.
(3) For lateral wind allowance. See Table 5.
(4) If obstruction exists between gun and target, and its highest point cannot be seen, ascertain if shots will clear by substituting "obstruction" for "own troops" in clearance column above, and find clearance by rule in Note (1). Minimum clearance required equals half height of cone for range to obstruction.

4th Field Survey Coy. R.E. 1633 27-7-17

Wharf Capt
Commdg 125th M.G. Coy

[P.T.O.

SECRET.   Appendix B   Copy No. 1

Operation Order No. M.
by
Captain G. E. Way
Comm'g "X" M.G. Coy at relieve said Company

REF. MAP   In the Field
1/10,000   21/12/17.
RICHEBOURG
LA BASSÉE
&
BÉTHUNE

1. The XXX Machine Gun Company will relieve the 177th Machine Gun Company in the line on the 23rd inst.

2. The Company will be divided as follows:—
   Right Group — 3 guns — under Lieut. A. J. Bainbridge and 2nd Lieut. Symes — with No. 1 Section, 1 gun of No. 2 Section under 2/Lt. Jones S.
   Left Group — 4 guns — Lieut. S. DICKINSON and No. 1 Section
   Battery Group — 7 guns — 2nd Lieut. W. W. STRAUSS and Lieut. E. B. GREENHALGH. No. 3 Section and 3 guns of No. 2 Section
   Right, Left and Battery Groups will relieve right, left and battery groups of 12th M.G. Company.

3. 12.30 a.m. B Oile.
   1.0 a.m. see fire Tea or Soup
   2.0 a.m. Coys be ready to move off:— Right, Left and Battery Groups. These will proceed to Coy Company H.Q. at F.26.3.6. where they will pick up guides to underlying points.
   Right Group will proceed to WINDY CORNER, A 5 c 82.32 arriving by 4.0 a.m. where own team guides will meet them
   Left and Battery Groups will proceed to MAISON CORNER A 16.7.38 the former arriving by 4 a.m., the latter by 4.15 a.m. Here team guides will meet Left Group, and one guide conduct Battery Group to Battery.

4. Headquarters will proceed and H moves off at 3.0 a.m. They will proceed to advanced Headquarters, taking up guides at Rear Headquarters.

Sheet 2

They will arrive at Advanced Headquarters, [illegible] by 8 a.m.
[illegible] Headquarters Limber when unloaded will be available
for use by 127th M.G. Company, also 2 limbers of Battery
Group when unloaded.

5. Transport and remainder of Company will move off at [illegible]
to Battery Company Headquarters under Transport Officer's
arrangements.
   Breakfast 6.45 a.m.

6. All maps, sketches, defence schemes, work [illegible] etc. will
be taken over on relief.
   Group Commanders will make arrangements for
exchanging their 1/10,000 [illegible] and 1/[illegible] [illegible] maps
for maps showing [illegible] positions.
   They will render to the Battery Group by 12 noon
[illegible], duplicate lists of all [illegible] stores etc. [illegible]
over.

7. Group Officers will reconnoitre their groups on [illegible] and
all will proceed [illegible] the time as the [illegible] unit,
arriving at Group Company Headquarters at [illegible] noon, [illegible]
to the relieved.
   [illegible] will acquaint himself with [illegible] [illegible]
arrangements and will [illegible] on completion of [illegible].

8. Relief complete will be reported by the code word "[illegible]"

9. ACTION at 6 a.m.

[signature]

[illegible handwritten notes at bottom]

SECRET.   Copy...7...

Appendix B.
W D

Administrative Instructions
by
Captain G.L. Hay
Issued with O.O. No. 10.

B.E.F. MAP
1/10000.
RICHEBOURG.
LA BASSÉE
&
BEUVRY.

In the Field
21/12/17.

1. Right and Left Groups will take over 8 boxes and belts, filled, per gun. They will hand 8 steel boxes and belts filled per gun to the L.M. Stores by 8 p.m. 22nd inst.

   Right Group will take in two belt filling machines and the Battery will take in two belt filling machines.

   Battery will take in 74 boxes and belts, filled per gun.

2. Surplus belt boxes (60) will be packed on ammunition limber accompanying Headquarters.

3. The usual gun equipment will be taken.

   Left and right groups will take two spare parts boxes each and Barrage Group three.

4. Sections will be accompanied by their fighting limbers to Rear Company Headquarters, where limbers not required will be left.

   Right Group. - The fore portion of one fighting limber will be packed with 5 guns, tripods etc., required for the line.

   Left Group. - The fore portion of one fighting limber will be packed with 4 guns, tripods etc., required for the line.

   Battery Group. - Three limbers taken with 7 guns, tripods, 112 belts and boxes etc., required for the line.

5. Rations for 23rd inst will be issued out at 4 p.m. same inst at L.M. Stores

   Rations for 24th and onwards will be made

Sheet 2.

teams and ration carriers will be sent to Company Headquarters daily at 4 p.m.

The G.S. Wagon will be available for rations on 22nd inst.

6. Headquarters limber will be packed with:—

    Front Ration { Orderly Room Stores
                  Signalling Kit.

    Rear Ration { 3 Officers Valises
                  Mess Stores

One S.A.A. Limber will be packed with 60 belt boxes on afternoon of 22nd by Nos 1 & 4 Sections. This limber will proceed with Headquarters and return to Rear Company Headquarters after unloading.

7. Two bicycles will be taken to Advanced Company Headquarters.

8. Communications:—

The following signallers will be at Company Headquarters. Ptes. Barker. W. Clayp H. and Bowley J.

    at Rear Company Headquarters. Cpl Dyson & Pte Walters.
    at Battery Group. Pte Mills E.

Allotment of Telephones:—

    Company Headquarters:— 1 F Telephone and 1 D III Telephones
    Rear Company Headquarters:— 1. Telephone.
    Battery Group. :— 1. Telephone.

Signallers will parade with their groups.

9. C.S.M. will act as guide to and lorry for the Company and S.A.B. at Town Major's office DETHUNE at 7 a.m. 2nd inst. Q.M.S. will see that one half of the lorry is loaded with stores on arrival.

G.S. Wagon and 3 limbers will report for loading at 9.30 a.m. 2nd inst. for loading with Stores.

These will proceed to Rear Company Headquarters and return after unloading.

One Storeman and 3 O.R. to be detailed by C.S.M. will parade .... lorry as unloading party. They will take rations .... inclusive and remain as guard over stores

Secret

10. The 2nd in Command will remain behind to hand over and obtain clean certificate.

11. All packs and blankets to handed in to Q.M. Stores at 12.30 Aug 2 23rd inst.

12. Dress.
    Great coats will be worn bandolier fashion over right shoulder.
    Leather jerkins will be carried on belt at back.

13. Orderly Sergeant will report when barracks are clean to 2nd in Command. Men left behind to be used in cleaning up.

Henry Captain,
Commanding 125th M.G. Company

Issued at 4hrs by orderly.
Copy to O.C. Right Group
"   "   "   "   Left   "
"   "   "   "   Battery
"   "   "   "   Transport
"   "   "   "   R.S.M.
"   "   "   "   Q.M.S.
"   "   "   "   War Diary
"   "   "   "   2nd in Command
"   "   "   "   File

Appendix C

Tactical and Technical Lessons learnt during Month.

I Tactical Lessons.

1. From experience gained on our present front, the sectors north and south of the LA BASSÉE canal, and also elsewhere it appears that there is a shortage of Vickers Guns. In order to economise guns as much as possible, and to enable them to be allocated where most required and to the best advantage, it is suggested that each Division should have a battalion of 48 Vickers Guns which would be Divisional Machine Guns.

   Surplus guns would be organised as Army Troops and kept in some central position so as to be available for any sudden contingency that might arise.

2. With especial reference to the same front it is submitted that defence in depth, the guns being located chequer-wise and covering one another, has been sacrificed in an attempt to form an infilade or oblique barrage, which only covers a proportion of the front, and owing to lack of guns lacks depth. The objection to a barrage in this case in addition, is that the trenches are nearer than 400 yards

and therefore from a technical point of view the jumping off point for the enemy cannot be successfully barraged without endangering our own troops. In addition where the trenches are very close probably the first intimation would be the presence of the enemy in our front line, in which case the barrage came down too late, though it is admitted that in an attack on a large scale supports would be caught to a certain extent.

It is suggested that guns should be distributed chequer-wise and mutually supporting as far as possible to a depth of 1000ᵡ to 1200ᵡ from our own front line.

Guns distributed like this would bring indirect fire to bear on selected points such as communication trenches, places of assembly in rear of enemy's lines etc., on the S.O.S. going up until required for close defence.

With reference to the present batteries it is improbable that there would be time to move the guns to mutually supporting close defence positions in depth over the Brigade front. They could only be formed into a strong point in the neighbourhood of the battery position which in itself might not be an ideal

3.

position for a strong point.

An attempt to scatter these guns would probably lead also to their detection.

3. Another point which affects the tactical situation indirectly is that it would increase the efficiency of a Company if it could get back its original men, when they have gone sick or wounded, on return to the duty, subject to the exigencies of the service. Recently this Company was below strength and applied for reinforcements. We asked for men previously in the Company, known to be at the Base Depot but the application was refused.

4. The usual difficulties have been experienced with regard to the under-establishment of a Machine Gun Company for working purposes, owing to the percentage of men sick, on leave, courses etc.

Usually the 16 Guns are all in the line for the full period for which the Brigade is in. Even when only 4 men per team are sent in with each gun it is not possible to work

4.

complete reliefs and no double sentries have to be found at night for the majority of the guns and a fair percentage of the guns usually do day and night firing the strain on the men is continuous

This state of affairs is unavoidable under existing conditions.

II Technical Lessons

1. Reference First Army Traversing Stops issued for trial. It is suggested that two pointers be issued with each stop instead of one, to enable a switch of 180° to be obtained. With only one pointer a traverse of more than 40° cannot be obtained without the arms of the crosshead coming in contact with the wing nuts of the stops, with the result that the left nut unscrews and the right nut tightens. The additional points would act quite as ~~such~~ satisfactory as the reading points for the traversing dial.

It is found that there is a tendency for the stops to move about 2° where the gun and crosshead is swung against the stops. The smooth metal

— 5 —

to metal contact does not give a
sufficient grip.

It is proposed to experiment
with a leather washer.

21/12/17.   (signed)   L. C. Kay,
                        Captain,
Commanding 125th M.G. Company.

Appendix D

Statement showing strength of Company Casualties etc.

	OFF.	O.R.
Strength of Company on Dec 1st 1917. (Including 1 officer and 17. O.R.)	12.	194
Drafts etc.		12.
	12.	206.

Casualties etc. OFF. O.R.

	OFF.	O.R.
Killed		2
Died of Wounds.		—
Wounded.		1
Wounded. Gas.		1
Wounded & Missing		—
Hospital		10.
Struck off Strength	1.	6.
	1.	20.

	OFF.	O.R.
	1.	20
Strength on January 1.st 1918. Including 1 officer & 17 O.R. attached.	11.	186.

	OFF.	O.R.
Numbers in Field Ambulance during month of December.		12.
" rejoined " " " "		2.
" proceeded on leave " " "	3.	11.
" rejoined from " " " "	2.	5.
" proceeded on duty to U.K " " " "		1
	5.	31

Horses etc in possession

	OFFICERS CHARGERS.	L.D. HORSES.	MULES
On December 1st 1917.	4.	31	15.
Evacuated During Month.	—		
Killed	—		
Wounded	—		
Sick 3.L.D.			
Cast 8.L.D. 2M.		11	2
	4.	20.	13.
Drawn during month.	3.	11	—
Present Strength.	7.	31	13.

APPENDIX E.

Machine Gun Dispositions
125th Machine Gun Company.

Identification Trace for use with Artillery Maps.

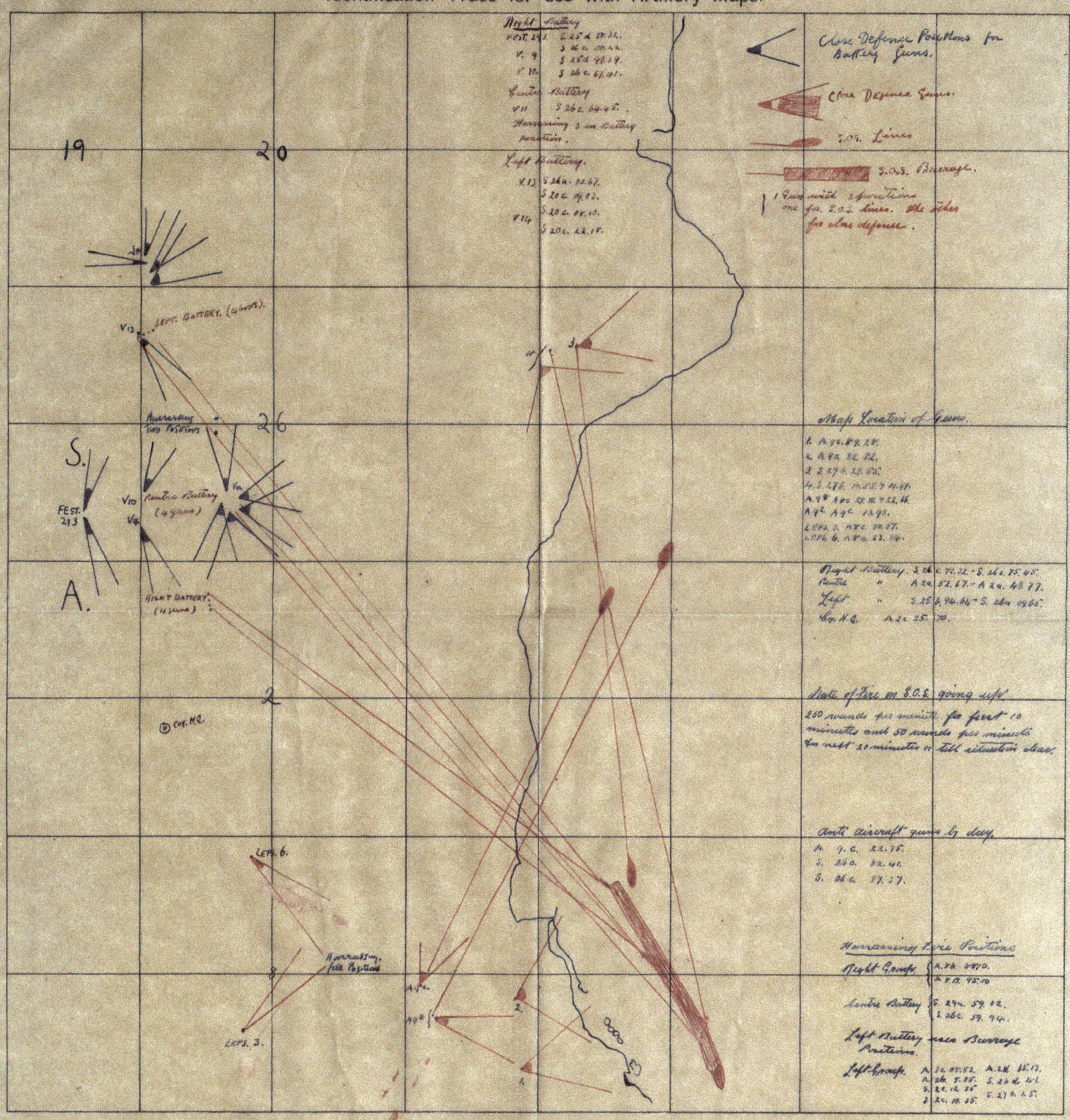

NOTE.—(1). These traces are intended to facilitate the communication of information as to the position of targets, which have been located on a squared map.
(2). The squares on this trace are 500 yards in length on the 1/10,000 scale, 1,000 yards in length on the 1/20,000 scale, and 2,000 yards in length on the 1/40,000 scale.
(3). The letters and numbers must also be added to enable the recipient to place the trace in the correct position on his own map. A little detail may also be traced, but this is not essential. The name and scale of the map to which the trace refers must be always given. The trace can be used for the 1/10,000, 1/20,000, or 1/40,000 scale.

G.S.G.S. 3025.

Tracing taken from Sheet 36 S.W.3 (••)

of the 1/10,000 map of LA BASSÉE
RICHEBOURG

Signature .... Date 7/12/17

Original.

Confidential

War Diary
for
125th Machine Gun Company
from
January 1st to January 31st
1918.

VOLUME XIII

Army Form C. 2118.

125 Coy M.G.C.
January 1918

WAR DIARY
or
INTELLIGENCE SUMMARY.
(Erase heading not required.)

Instructions regarding War Diaries and Intelligence Summaries are contained in F. S. Regs., Part II. and the Staff Manual respectively. Title pages will be prepared in manuscript.

Place	Date 1918	Hour	WEATHER	Summary of Events and Information	Remarks and references to Appendices
FRANCE Ref Map. BC.N.W.1. LA BASSEE 1/10,000	Jan 1st		Fair. Wind E. mild. Visibility good.	5 guns fired 5000 rounds on targets at A10c 90.94. A4B 30.63. A4c 35.54. A4b 49.7 and S29a.14. Lieut Webb. U.S.A. attached for instruction.	AAC
36 S.W.3 RICHEBOURG 1/10,000	Jan 2nd		Dull. Thaw. Wind. Mild N.W. Frost at night	6 guns fired 6000 rounds on targets at A4c 35.40 A4b 30.63 A4d 00.30. A5c 00.60 S28c 70.57 S29 a. 31.70.	AAC
	Jan 3rd		Sunny. Fine. Cold. Visibility very good. Wind mild N.E.	6 guns fired 6000 rounds on targets at A4c 42.39 A10c 79.86 ↊ S28b 68.68 Lt Webb hit by carriers.	AAC
	Jan 4th		Fair. Visibility very poor No wind.	Divisional Commander inspected 125 MG Coy in the line. 6 guns fired 6000 rounds on targets at A10c 52.73 A4c 50.94 A4c 42.79. A4d 72.12 A4d 72.12 S29a 15.55	AAC
	Jan 5th		Dull Visibility poor. Wind. mild. West. Frost at night.	6 guns fired 6000 rounds on targets at A10c 90.44 · A5c 00.60 · A4c 35.50 · A4b 30.63 · A4b 65.01 · S25d 85.22	AAC
	Jan 6th		Dull visibility poor. Wd mild S.E. Frost at night	6 guns fired 6000 rounds on targets at A4c 65.35 A4B 30.60 S28b 92.12 A11c 90.44 A11a 85.52 A4c 30.62. Centre Batts inspected Range 2500. OFL 1500. Reserve clearance 50 Ft in path	AAC
	Jan 7th		Damp Raw Cold. Visibility poor. Wind fresh N.	6 guns fired 6000 rounds on targets at A5a 14.14. A17a 86.90 S29 c 00.50 A4c 35.50 A4b 30.63 A4c 49.96. Col Coulson A.S.C. inspected Transport lines	AAC
	Jan 8th		Snowed. Wind strong N Visibility very poor. West	6 guns fired 6000 rounds on targets at A10c 94.84 A4d 15.92 A4b 45.60 S28 c 94.15 A4a 49.67 A4a 01.24. (or)	AAC

1577 Wt.W10791/1773 500,000 1/15 D.D.&L. A.D.S.S./Forms/C. 2118.

Army Form C. 2118.

WAR DIARY
or
INTELLIGENCE SUMMARY.
(Erase heading not required.)

175 Coy, M.G.C.
January. 1918.

Instructions regarding War Diaries and Intelligence Summaries are contained in F.S. Regs., Part II. and the Staff Manual respectively. Title pages will be prepared in manuscript.

Place	Date 1918	Hour	Summary of Events and Information	Weather	Remarks and references to Appendices
FRANCE Ref Map 36cNW1 LA BASSÉE 1/10000 36.SW3 RICHEBOURG 1/10000	Jan. 8th (Cont)		No 1 Sect (from Rt Batts) relieved No 3 Sect (in Lt group) to Lt Batts. Two guns from LGPS 3a LGPS 6 relieved 2 guns in Lt group - to LGPS 3 & 6. Lieut H.A. Sale M.C. rejoined from leave to U.K. Officers commanding groups are: Rt GROUP 2/Lt W.A. HARRISON. LEFT GROUP Lt. C.R. GREENHALGH. Rt. BATTY Lt H.A. SALE M.C. CENTRE BATTY 2/Lt W.M. STRAWSON. LGFT BATTY Lt T MILLS (126 Co). NCO i/c LEPS guns Sgt Lawlor W.		ADC
	Jan. 9th		6 guns fired 6000 rounds on targets at. A4c X5 45 A9a70 35 A4c 62-23. A10B 50 31. A11c 90-44 S29a 3075.	Fine at first. Dull later. Visibility good at first but bad late. Wind strong N.W.	ADC
	Jan. 10th		1 OR wounded by shell fire. 6 guns fired 6000 rounds on targets at A10c 96 68. A11a 58 32. A4c 65 35. A4b 36 50 A10 a 70·80. S28b 68 68. LIEUT. S. DICKINSON proceeded on 14 days' leave to U.K.	Dull. Visibility bad. Wind fresh NW. Continued thaw.	ADC
	Jan. 11th		6 guns fired 6000 rounds on targets at A4c 56 34. A4c 42 39. A10d 65 53. A2 d5 6 83. A4c 31 45. S28d 61 51.	Dull - Rain. Windrose N W. Visibility v. poor.	ADC
	Jan. 12th		6 guns fired 8000 rounds on targets at S28c 47 15. A4c 20 70. S28B 92-33. A4d 65·05. A40 60 53. S26 c 59 94	Dull. Thaw Cont. Mild W. Visibility poor	ADC
	Jan. 13th		7 guns fired 7000 rounds on targets at A4d 65 05. A4c 31 45. A4a 94 65. S26d 18 56. A7a 40 94. A10b 45 57. S28B 95. 64	Dull. Thaw too warm. Visibility. Fair.	ADC
	Jan. 14th		6 guns fired 6000 rounds on targets at A4b 72 00. A10a 90 28. S29a 12 US. A4c 65 35 A4b 35-66 A4c 3062.	Dull. Snow No wind. Visibility very bad.	ADC

Army Form C. 2118.

125 Coy M.G.C.
January 1918

WAR DIARY
or
INTELLIGENCE SUMMARY.
(Erase heading not required.)

Instructions regarding War Diaries and Intelligence Summaries are contained in F. S. Regs., Part II. and the Staff Manual respectively. Title pages will be prepared in manuscript.

Place	Date 1918	Hour	Summary of Events and Information	Remarks and references to Appendices
FRANCE Ref Maps 36c NW1	Jan 15th		WEATHER. Full Thaw. Rain. Wind fresh west. visibility poor	6 guns fired 6000 rounds on targets at A9a 9465 S28d 1850 A9c 7057 A10d 6153 A9d 3683 A4b 8070
LA BASSÉE 1/10,000 36 SW 3	Jan 16th		Heavy rain. Wind fresh west. visibility bad.	Left Batts wired to positions at 7 guns fired 7000 rounds on targets at A9c 5045 S28d 1850 A9a 4969 S29a 0930 A4b 7200 A9c 9739 S28b 9564
RICHEBOURG 1/10,000 36A SE 36 S.W 36 b NE 36 NW 1/40,000	Jan 17th		Rain. Visibility poor. wind west.	6 guns fired 6000 rounds on targets at A4b 7200 A10a 9028 A9c 6025 A4b 35.60 A9c 28.46 S29a 10.40 2/Lieut W.A.HARRISON to M.C.C.S. (sick) 7 guns 126 MG coy in left Batt, relieved by no 5 sect 125 MG coy from R/ Batt. 126 Sect to R/ Batt. M. coy
BETHUNE C 81.6 1/40,000	Jan 18th	6.30 am		125 MGCoy less one sect. (in left Batt) relieved by 126 MG coy. Relief complete 6 am. Appendix "A" Coy marched to 6 Gilletes at ESSARS. Arrived ESSARS. 8 am. Relief orders
		3 pm -10 midnight		1 officer & 50 O.R. taking working party a VILLAGE LINE.
	Jan 19th	am 7.30 -12 noon 3pm -10pm		Bathing - Cleaning - Kit inspection etc 1 Officer & 50 O.R working party a Village Lines
	Jan 20th	9 am 3 pm -6 pm		Church Parade. (Voluntary) 1 officer & 50 O.R working party a VILLAGE LINE
	Jan 21st	7 am 8.30 am -4 pm 3 pm -10 pm		Rouse Parade Washing clothes - Issue of kit deficiencies - fatigues at transport lines for inspection & treatment 1 officer & 40 O.R working party on VILLAGE LINE

1577 Wt. W10791/1773 500,000 1/15 D.D. & L. A.D.S.S./Forms/C. 2118.

WAR DIARY
or
INTELLIGENCE SUMMARY.
(Erase heading not required.)

Army Form C. 2118.

125 Coy M.G.C.
January 1918.

Place	Date 1918	Hour	Summary of Events and Information	Remarks and references to Appendices
FRANCE Ref Maps 36A SE 36 SW 36B NE 36C NW BETHUNE EDT. 6. 1/40,000	Jan. 22nd	7 am 8.30-11.30 11.30 3 pm	Rouse Parade. Building mud walls at Transport lines. Checking & inspection of gun stores etc. Inspection of Coy Officers (less Transport) by C.O. 1 Offr & 90 O.R. working party on VILLAGE LINE.	HAC
	Jan. 23rd	7.15 am 8.30 am 9 am-12 n 3 pm	Rouse Parade. Saluting Drill – Gas drill. Boots, wg & Squad drill. 1 Offr & 40 O.R. working party on VILLAGE LINE.	HAC
	Jan. 24th	7 am 8.30-9.30 9.45-12.15 3 pm 10 pm	Rouse Parade. Inspection of Coy (less Transport) by C.O. Saluting Drill. Gas Drill. Inspection of Coy by Medical Officer. Building mud walls etc. at Transport lines. 1 Offr & 40 O.R. working party on VILLAGE LINE. No 4 Sect (Lieut A.C. Herridge) relieved No 3 Sect (Lieut H.A. Sale) attached to 126 M.G.Coy in the line. Relief complete 10.30 pm. Same attacht done.	HAC
	Jan. 25th	7 am 8.30-9.30 9.30-12.15 2.30 pm 3 pm	Rouse Parade. Inspection of Coy (less Transport) by C.O. Saluting Drill – Gas drill. Squad drill. Working party on mud walls at Transport lines. Inspection of Transport by C.O. 40 O.R. working party on VILLAGE LINE. Lieut S. DICKINSON returned from 14 days leave to U.K.	HAC
	Jan. 26th	7 am 8.30-9.30 9.30-12.15 3 pm	Rouse Parade. Inspection by Section Officers. Saluting Drill – Squad Drill. Parade of Coy under Div Gas Officer. Lecture – Drill & Practice in gas helmets with guns in smoke cloud. Working party to men at Transport lines Gathering. 40 O.R. working party on VILLAGE LINE.	HAC
	Jan. 27th	?	Reconnoitred line held by 127th Infantry Brigade. Church parades. Working party on VILLAGE LINE, 40 O.R.	mello

1577 Wt. W10791/1773 500,000 1/15 D.D.&L. A.D.S.S./Forms/C. 2118.

WAR DIARY
or
INTELLIGENCE SUMMARY.
(Erase heading not required.)

125 Coy. M.G.C.
January 1918.

Army Form C. 2118.

Instructions regarding War Diaries and Intelligence Summaries are contained in F. S. Regs., Part II. and the Staff Manual respectively. Title pages will be prepared in manuscript.

Place	Date 1918	Hour	Summary of Events and Information	Remarks and references to Appendices
FRANCE Ref. Maps. 36A.SE 36.SW 36B.NE 36C.NW BETHUNE E. Dt. 6. 1/40,000.	JAN. 28	7.0am 8.0am–9.10am 9.10am–9.20am 9.20am 11.30am 12.30pm 2.pm–4.30pm	Rouse parade. Inspection under Section Officers. Saluting Drill. Company Parade for Baths, at BETHUNE. Cleaning guns, spare parts, etc. Walking party at Transport lines on mud walls etc. Capt. H.B. CARL 15 L.E. on leave to U.K.	Appendix "B" Relief Orders Passes
	JAN. 29	9.0am–9.15am 9.15am–9.25am 9.25am–9.40am Remainder of day.	Sec. 1. Proceeded into line with 127 M.G. Coy. Section officers reconnoitred line. Company Inspection. Gas Transport. Saluting Drill. Gas Drill. Preparation for line.	Passes
	JAN. 30	Weather cold + misty	Relieved the 127th Company Machine Gun Corps in the line, CANAL SECTOR. LIEUT. L. SMITH injured from Leave to U.K. 2000 rounds harassing fire on target A.22.6.70.45 and A.23.c.50.05.	Passes
	JAN. 31	Weather cold + misty	Fired 2000 rounds harassing fire on target A.23.c A.2.70 and A.23.a.40.63.	Passes

Attached are the following: Tactical & Technical Lessons learnt during the month. Important Messages.

Appendix "C" Appendix "D"

T. Wing Captain,
Commanding 125 M.G. Company
1/2/18.

Appendix A.

Operation Orders No 14.
By Captain C. C. Day.
Commanding R.4.R.E.

Secret.
13-1-18.

1. The 125 M.G. Coy will be relieved by the 126 M.G. Coy in the GIVENCHY SECTOR on the 16th inst, in accordance with attached relief and march table.

2. All Trench Stores, A.A. Positions, maps, Defence Schemes, Schemes of work and wiring in progress and projected, & documents relating to this Sector including aero-plane photographs, will be handed over on relief. Receipted lists for such stores will be handed in to the Orderly Room by 6 p.m. 16th inst.

3. 14 belt boxes and belts filled in good condition will be handed over per gun on relief. The 2nd I/C will take over 72 boxes bulk S.A.A. and 4000 for practice and 224 belt boxes and belts filled at ESSARS from 126 M.G. Coy and the C.Q.M.S. will hand over 72 boxes bulk S.A.A. at GORRE and obtain receipt for same.

4. Group and Battery Officers will ensure that all dug-outs etc are handed over in a clean and sanitary condition and receipts obtained.

5. Officers of 126 M.G. Coy will reconnoitre line on 15th inst. Arrangements for guides for them to be notified later.

6. Groups, Batteries and Coy H.Q. will each have 1 guide at RATION CORNER for their limbers as follows :- 1 guide from LEPS 3 or 6 for No 1 Section limber at 5-25.a.m. to take limber to WINDY CORNER. 1 guide from Centre Battery for No 4 Section half limber at 5-15.a.m. 1 guide from Left Group for No 2 Section half limber at 5-45.A.M. 1 guide from Coy H.Q. for 2 limbers @ 5-45.a.m.

7. 126 M.G. Coy will ration 1 Section of 125 M.G. Coy total 21 and men garrisoning keeps, total 28 from 17th inst inclusive. These numbers will be struck off the Ration Strength of 125 M.G. Coy after the 16th inst inclusive.

8. Relief complete will be reported to Advanced Coy H.Q. in writing by runner by the CODEWORD SLUDGE. Centre Battery & Left Group may report by same codeword by wire when ready to move off.

9. ACKNOWLEDGE :-

Issued to:-
Copy No - 1. 2nd War.
        - 2. 5th Div.
        - 3. Hill.
        - 4. O.C. Right Group
        - 5. - Left -
        - 6. - Right Batty.

Copy No 7 O.C. Centre Batty
    - 8. - Left -
    - 9. - O.C 126th Coy
    - 10. C.Q.M.S.

J. C. Day
Captain
Commanding R.4.R.E.

Secret

Appendix B.

Ref map 1/10000 LA BASSÉE
  "   "   "   RICHEBOURG.

Operation Orders no 15.
By
Captain A. C. Kay
Commanding 125th M. G. Coy.

Copy No. 9

In The Field
28-1-18

1. The 125th Machine Gun Coy will relieve the 127th Machine Gun Company in the line on the forenoon of the 30th instant. Relief will be conducted as per attached relief and march table.

2. The Company will be divided into four groups, A. B. C. and D, as shown in appendix A.

3. Group Officers will reconnoitre the line on the 29th instant.

    Lieut A. L. Herridge — A. Group.
    Lieut H. A. Salt. M.C. — B. Group.
    2nd Lieut W. H. Strawson — C. Group. will be at PONT FIXE and
    Lieut S. Dickinson — D. Group at T. Road,
A20d 18.45. at 9.30. a.m. 29th instant, where guides will meet them. They will be accompanied by the Nos. 1 of their Groups, who will remain in the line. Nos 1 will take 1 days rations and unexpended portion of rations for 29th inst.

4. All French maps, and French stores, Aeroplane photographs, and calculations, positions, schemes and work in progress will be taken over on relief. Lists of all stores taken over will be handed in to the Orderly Room by 6. p.m. 30th inst.

5. Relief complete will be wired by A. B & C. Groups from A. Group. H.Q, and by D. Group through Right Battalion H.Q. by code word. KITTY.

6. ACKNOWLEDGE.

Copies To:—
No 1 " OC. A. Group.
 - 2 "   B   "
 - 3 "   C   "
 - 4 "   D   "
 - 5 " I. O.
 - 6 " C. S. M.
 - 7 " C. Q. M. S.
 - 8 " OC 127 M. G. Coy.
 - 9 " W. D.

A. C. Kay, Captain
Commanding 125 M. G. Coy.

Serial No.	Date.	Unit.	To Relieve.	From.	To.	Route.	Guides.	Remarks.
1.	30th.	B. Coys. R.S.R. & Attchd. V.G. Section 1 Gun to 9 R.B. Gun. No. 4 Redan.	A. Coy. 6 Guns 127th. G. Coy.	ESSARS	Post Fire George.	L.E. HAMEL, QUEEN RAMPART, DISPR. L.E. PKW. — CANAL — PONT-FIXE.	Post Fire 8-30 a.m.	½ Ration Reserve left 8-30 a.m. Several Pack Lusitania Rockets to Pont-Fixe closed to wheeled traffic. Limber taking to transport lines L.E. PKW.
2.	30th.	B. Coys. 2nd. E. Lancashire 3 Guns to 9 R.B. Section.	B. Group 3 Guns 127th. G. Coy.	do.	BRICKSTACKS.	do.	do.	1 Limber leave off 6-30 a.m. Canal Road Pont Fixe & Festubert to Pont Fixe closed to wheeled traffic. Limber return to transport lines L.E. PKW.
3.		C. Coys. 2nd. E. Lancashire 4 Guns to 9 R.B. Section.	C. Group 3 Guns 127th. G. Coy.	do.	HUNT VIEW Group.	do.	do.	do.
4.	30th.	D. Coys. 2nd. E. Lancashire 9 R.B. Section.	D. Group 4 Guns 127th. G. Coy.	do.	V. & P. Roads.	CROIX-BARBÉE Canal at Transport Lines L.E. Battn. PROVOST AND OFFICER Richebourg to CAMBRIN.	Junction Harley St. & Riggers Road A.388/1944 8-30 a.m.	1 Limber leave off 6.15 a.m. Limbers return to Transport Lines L.E. PKW.
5.	30th.	Hqrs. Same Plans Transport.	Hqrs. 8 for Transport. 127th. G. Coy.	do.	L.E. PKW.	See also Remarks re. 3. & 4. L.E. PKW.		Limber leave off 9-30 a.m. From L. ESSARS.

2 OC types Assistant Letters Group

125 Bde.   Appendix C
Tactical & Technical Lessons learnt during the Month.

1. **Tactical.**
  Nothing to report.

2. **Technical**
  During the recent frosty weather the allowance of 1 pint of glycerine residue per gun ~~per gun~~ was found to be insufficient to prevent the gun from freezing.
  It is suggested that the allowance should be 4 pints per gun, 2 pints to be in the gun and 2 kept in reserve in frosty weather. There appears to be no doubt that the solution becomes de-natured with use and a reserve is necessary owing to the length of time it takes to get supplies.

  (Signed) G.C. Kay. Captain,
  Cmdg. 125 M.G.Co.

G.K.67
17/1/18.

Appendix D

Statement shewing strength of Company, Casualties &c.

	OFFS.	O.R.
Strength of Company on 1st January 1918. (Including 1 Officer & 17 O.R. attached)	11	186
Drafts &c. (includes 3 O.R. attached)	–	7
	11	193

Less Casualties:

	OFF.	O.R.
Killed.		1
Died of wounds.		1
Wounded.		–
Wounded – Gas.		–
Wounded & Missing.		–
Hospital		7
Struck off strength. (includes 1 attached off.)	2	6

	OFFS.	O.R.
	2	15
Strength at 1st February 1918. (including 16 O.Rs attached)	9	178
No. in Field ambulance during month of Jany.	1	13
" rejoined from .		5
" proceeded on leave.	1	11
" rejoined from leave.	3	12
" proceeded on duty to U.K.		2

Horses etc in possession.

	Officers Chargers	L.D. Horses	Mules.
Strength at 1st January 1918.	7	31	13
Less Evacuated during month of Jany.			
Killed			
Wounded			
Sick			
Cast.		4	
	7	27	13
Drawn during month of January.	–	5	3
	7	32	16

Confidential

War Diary
for
125th Machine Gun Company
from
February 1st to February 28th
1918.

Volume XIV

WAR DIARY

INTELLIGENCE SUMMARY

(Erase heading not required.)

125 COY. M.G.C.

February 1918.

Army Form C. 2118.

Place	Date	Hour	WEATHER	Summary of Events and Information	Remarks and references to Appendices
FRANCE Ref. Maps 1/10000 36cNW 1/40000 36 A.S.E. 36 S.W. 36 B.N.E. 36 C.N.W. LA BASSÉE & BETHUNE.	1918 Feb. 1.		Foggy - Wind mild E. - Slight frost.	Our machine guns fired 2000 rounds on targets A23a 40.63. and A23c 82.70.	appendix E.
	Feb. 2		Foggy, later clear, slight frost - wind mild S.E.	Our machine guns fire 2000 rounds on targets A23a 58.06 and A23c 67.68.	nil
	Feb. 3.		Wind mild S.E. - clear & cloudy by turns.	Two of our machine guns fired 2000 rounds on target A23b 15.80 and A26 70.45.	nil
	Feb. 4		Clear & cloudy by turns - wind mild S.E.	Our machine guns fired 2000 rounds on target A23a 48.65. 2nd A17c 72.44	nil
	Feb. 5.		Bright - wind mild S.E.	Harassing guns fired 2000 rounds on A17c 42.13/8 and A23c 70.95.	nil
	Feb. 6.		Bright - wind mild S.E.	Our guns fired 2000 rounds on targets A23 bd 26.80 and A22 d 40.85.	nil
	Feb. 7.		Cloudy & showery Wind mild S.E.	Harassing guns fired 2000 rounds on targets A29 b 34.56 and A26 70.45.	nil
	Feb. 8		Cloudy - wind strong S.	Our guns fired 2000 rounds on targets A23a 70.20. and A23a 70.30.	nil
	Feb. 9		Cloudy - wind fresh S.W.	Our machine guns fired 2000 rounds on targets A29 a 54.52 and X roads A23a 40.63.	nil
	Feb. 10		Wind strong S.W.	Our guns fired 2000 rounds on targets A29 b 22.6c and A29 b 18.86.	nil

Army Form C. 2118.

125th Coy. M.G.C.
February 1918.

WAR DIARY
INTELLIGENCE SUMMARY
(Erase heading not required.)

Instructions regarding War Diaries and Intelligence Summaries are contained in F. S. Regs., Part II. and the Staff Manual respectively. Title pages will be prepared in manuscript.

Place	Date 1918	Hour	WEATHER	Summary of Events and Information	Remarks and references to Appendices
FRANCE. Ref. Map. 1/10000 36cNW1. LA BASSÉE	Feb. 11.		Cloudy - slight rain & wind SW. fresh.	Our machine guns fired 2000 rounds on targets A.29.a. 10.B2.C (Track) and trench A17.c 72. 44. S.O.S. lines tested.	Appx B
	Feb. 12.		Wind - fresh SW - Cloudy.	Our machine guns harassed targets A.23.a.2.4 and footbridge over canal at A.17.c.4.2.38.	Appx B
	Feb. 13.		Wind - mild SW cloudy & draggy.	Our machine guns harassed targets A.17.c.72.44 (trench) and A.23.d. 57.82 (Track).	Appx B
	Feb. 14.		Wind - fresh SW - raining.	Our machine guns fired 2000 rounds on targets A17.c 27.16 (Stalk) and A.2.3.a.57.06 (Regt.H.B). Nos. 1 of 164 inf. Coy. proceeded into line.	Appx B
H40000 (36A S.E. 36 S.W. 36 B.N.E. 36 C.N.W.	Feb. 15.		Cloudy - mild SW Wind.	Relieved in the line by 164 M.G. Coy. marched on completion of relief to L'ABEUVRIÈRE. (Appendix.A) Captain M.B. CARLISLE rejoined from leave to U.K.	Appendix A
	Feb. 16.	9am - 12 noon		Bathing. Cleaning kit equipment etc.	
	Feb. 17.	9am -		Church Parade. Washing & cleaning equipment. Pay. 65964 Sgt. Arey P. MM appointed a/CSM vice 39565 Sgt. Gresty D. D.CM	Appx C
	Feb. 18.	9a-12noon 2p-4pm		Section & Company Inspection - Cleaning Lewis guns - NCO's Drill Kit Inspection by Section. NCO's BF & PT.	Appx C

WAR DIARY
INTELLIGENCE SUMMARY
(Erase heading not required.)

Army Form C. 2118.

125 Coy M.G.C.
February 1918.

Place	Date 1918	Hour	Summary of Events and Information	Remarks and references to Appendices
FRANCE A1/40 b 00 36 A.SE. 36 B S.W. 36 B NE 36 C NW	Feb 19	9a-11am 11-12:30 2-4:30	Company Inspection. Steady Drill Saluting. Demonstration of (proof) Gas Drill - Guard mounting. Demonstration of Barrage Drill a Pack saddlery drill. Barrage Drill. Lecture. (Capt Tillie M.C.) 1 one of kit deficiencies.	App C
	Feb 20	9a-10am 10a-12noon 2pm	Company Inspection. Steady Drill. Saluting Demonstration of Guard Mounting etc. Barrage Drill. Demonstration by Sect Officers of Laying out Barrage by Compass. Football – Games etc. CAPT. R.A. HELPS MC appointed 2nd in Command 42nd M.G. Bn. Lt R. RATYS BOTTOM – 2/Lt F.C. HATTERSON – Transport officer	App C
	Feb 21	9a-10am 10-12 2pm-3pm	Demonstration of Guard mounting. Drill & Saluting. Steady drill - handling of arms. Barrage Drill. (Demonstration by Sect Officers as on 20th) Pack saddlery drill. 4pm NCO's under Sgt Inst? Each Section 1/2 hr steady drill under Sgt Inst? during the day. Lt S. Dickinson proceeded as a Rifle Grenade Course at HURIONVILLE.	App C
	Feb 22	9am-9:30 9:30-1pm 2pm-3pm	Demonstration Steady Drill - Guard mounting and Saluting. Steady Drill. Barrage Drill (usual demonstration by Sec Offs) - Elementary gun drill. Physical Training Lecture on Sanitation by M.O. Address by C.O. Elementary Squad under Lt J.A. Cutter + Sgt Oates Trimer 4pm NCO's under Sgt Inst?	App C
	Feb 23	9am-11am 12-2 2-4pm	Company Inspection. Gas Drill I.A. Elementary Squad as usual. Saluting Football etc. Lt J.L. SMITH transferred to 31st M.G. Bn. (proceeded).	App C
	Feb 24	9:30 am	Church Parade.	App C
	Feb 25	9a-10am 10-12:45 2-3pm	Company Inspection. Steady Drill. Saluting. Gas Drill. Mechanism Stripping Stoppages. Barrage Drill. Company Parade. Drill under Sgt Inst? 4pm NCO's under Sgt Inst? Elementary Squad as usual.	App C

WAR DIARY
or
INTELLIGENCE SUMMARY.
(Erase heading not required.)

Army Form C. 2118.

125 Coy M.G.C.
February 1918.

Place	Date 1918	Hour	Summary of Events and Information	Remarks and references to Appendices
FRANCE Ref. Map. 1/40,000 36A.SE 36A.S.W. 36B.N.E. 36c.N.W.	Feb. 26.	8am to 6pm	Field Scheme in localities of VERMELLES, ANNEQUIN & SAILLY LA BOURSE. (see Appendix B attached). Remainder of Coy P.T. & Drill under Sgt. Instr. & Transport Fatigues. Elementary class as usual.	Appendix B
	Feb. 27	9am-11am 11-12.15pm	Inspection of A Coy by O.C. Coy. Steady Drill Saluting - Demonstration of Guard mounting. Drill under Sgt. Instr. - Lecture by Sect. Officers. 12.30 Lecture on Gas Service. Elementary class as usual.	#C
	Feb. 28.	9am-10am 11am-1pm 2pm-4pm	P.T. & Drill under Sgt. Instr. 10am Inspection of C Coy by O.C. Bn. Elementary fire direction. Practice in Guard mounting. Cleaning gun tackle - Mounting of arms & Guard mounting. Inspection of gun instr. testbook & rangefinder by Armourer Sgt. (A.O.C.) L.S. DICKINSON returned from course at HURONVILLE	#K #E

Attached are :-

APPENDIX A. Operation Order No. 76 & Administrative Instructions.
  "   B. Reinforcement Scheme.
  "   C. Technical & Tactical lesson.
  "   D. Monthly strength.
  "   E. Map &c.

[signature]
Lt. 125 MGC
1/3/18.

Secret. APPENDIX A. Copy No 10

Operation Orders No 6
by
Capt. G. C. Kay.
Commanding 125th. Machine Gun Company

Ref. Maps. 1:40000 Combined Sheet.   Field.
BETHUNE.   12/2/1918

1. The 125th. M.G. Company will be relieved in the line by the 164th. M.G. Company on 15th. inst. in accordance with attached march and time table.

2. On relief the 125th. M.G. Coy will proceed to LA BEUVRIERE.

3. All trench and area Stores, Defence Schemes, Aeroplane photos, maps (as detailed in M95 dated 11/2/1918), sketches, schemes of work in progress etc. will be handed over on relief. Receipts in duplicate will be obtained and handed to Adjutant on arrival at LE PREOL.

4. Administrative instructions will be issued separately.

5. Completion of relief will be reported to C.O. in person on arrival at LE PREOL.

6. No. 1 of 164 M.G. Coy. will proceed into line along with rations on 14th inst.

7. 64 belts - boxes per gun will be handed over to 164 M.G. Coy in the line. C.S.M. will take over 224 belts - boxes from 164 M.G. Coy at LE PREOL.

8. ACKNOWLEDGE

                      Kay Captain.
                      Commanding 125. M.G. Coy.

Issued to by Orderly.

Copy No. 1   D.M.G.O
" 2   C. of A Group
" 3   " B "
" 4   " C "
" 5   " D "
" 6   T.O.
" 7   O.C. No N.C.C.
" 8   C.Q.M.S.
" 9   S.M.
" 10   W.D.
" 11   W.D.
" 12   File.

March and Relief Table to accompany 125 M.G. Coy operation order No.16.

Serial No.	Date.	Unit.	From.	To.	Relieved by	Route.	Remarks.
1	15/2/18	A Group (4 guns) 125 M.G. Coy	LINE	LA BEUVRIERE	4 guns Section H.Q. 164 M.G.Coy	Via LE PREOL	1 guide from Bry H.Q. will guide 4 guns 164 M.G.Coy to Junction HARLEY St. — LA BASSEE main road A 20 d. 20. 50, leaving LE PREOL at 10 a.m. 1 guide from team and Section H.Q. A Group to be at above road Junction A.20 d.20.50 at 10.30 a.m. to guide in relieving teams and Section H.Q.
2	15/2/18	B. Group (4 guns) 125. M.G.Coy.	—do—	—do—	4 guns & Section H.Q. 164. M.G.Coy.	—do—	1 G.S. limbered wagon 125 M.G. Coy. will be at Rd. Junction A.20 d.20.50 at 11.30 a.m. to convey guns & Kits of A Group to LE PREOL. 1 guide from Bry H.Q. will guide 3 guns 164 M.G.Coy to PONT FIXE A.14.d.20.80 leaving LE PREOL at 10.0 a.m. 1 guide from team and Section H.Q. B Group to be at PONT FIXE at 10.30 a.m. to guide in relieving teams & Section H.Q.
3	15/2/18	C. Group (4 guns) 125 M.G.Coy.	—do—	—do—	4 guns & Section H.Q. 164 M.G.Coy	—do—	1. G.S. limbered wagon 125. M. & Coy. will be at PONTFIXE at 11.30 a.m. to convey guns and kits of B. Group to LE PREOL. 1 guide from Bry H.Q. will guide 4 guns 164 M.G. Coy to PONTFIXE A.14.d.20.80 leaving LE PREOL at 10 a.m. 1 guide from team and Section H.Q. C. Group to be at PONTFIXE at 10.30 a.m. to guide in relieving teams and Section H.Q.
4	15/2/18	D. Group 6 guns 125 M.G.Coy.	—do—	—do—	5 guns & Section H.Q. 164 M.G.Coy	—do—	1. G.S. limbered wagon 125. M.G. Coy. will be at PONT FIXE at 11.30 a.m. to convey guns and kits of C. Group to LE PREOL. 1 guide from Bry H.Q. will guide 4 guns 164 M.G.Coy to PONT FIXE at 10.0 a.m. 1 guide from team and Section H.Q. D. Group to be at PONT FIXE at 10.30 a.m. to guide in relieving teams & Section H.Q. 2 G.S. limbered wagons 125 M.G. Coy will be at PONT FIXE at 11.30 a.m. to convey guns and kit of D Group to LE PREOL.
5.	15/2/18	A.B.C. & D Groups Details by H.Q.	LE PREOL	—do—	—	—	Will march under C.O. at hour to be decided later.
6	15/2/18	Transport Trg N.O. Field details	—do—	—do—	—	—	Will march under T.O. to leave LE PREOL at 9.45 a.m.

Note:- (1) E. of LE PREOL an interval of 200ˣ between groups will be maintained.
(2) W. " " " " 100ˣ " " " "
ˣ Inclusive Transport & M.G. Section.

Secret.   APPENDIX B.   Copy No. 10

125th Machine Gun Company   WD
Administrative Instructions No 6.
Issued in conjunction with O.O. 6.

12th February 1918

1. TRANSPORT.

C.Q.M.S. will arrange to send G.S. Wagon loaded with surplus baggage to LA BEUVRIERE on 14th inst, also a G.S. limbered wagon with fuel. Pte Davies E. will accompany these and remain there as guards over stores and fuel. L.S.M. will detail two brakesmen to accompany G.S. Wagon & G.S. limbered wagon. These will return with wagons to LEPREOL on 14th inst. on completion of duty.

One motor lorry for this company will report at the CHATEAU LE QUESNOY at 8.0 am 15th inst. C.Q.M.S. will have a guide at above place at 8.0 am 15th inst. to guide lorry to Q.M. Stores.

H.Q's G.S. limbered wagon will report at Orderly Room at 8.0 am 15th inst, and will be loaded with Orderly Room stores. It will then proceed as near Signal Office as possible and be loaded with all Signalling stores, less instruments required until relief is complete. When loaded this limber will immediately report to Transport Officer.

No 12 G.S. limbered wagon will report at Q.M. Stores at 8.0 am and will be loaded with cooks tackle and rations required for Transport & H.Q. Sections proceeding at 9.45 a.m. It will also be loaded with tea ration for whole Company.

Officers Mess Cart will remain behind and proceed with company under C.O's orders later in the day. It will be loaded with Officers Mess Stores and remainder of Cooks tackle.

2. MEALS.

C.Q.M.S. will arrange for a hot dinner for A, B, C & D Groups and details of Coy. H.Q. at 1.0 p.m.

2

He will also send on one Cook with Transport at
9.45 a.m. to cook dinner for that party, and to have
tea ready for Company on arrival at LA BEUVRIERE
from 4.0 p.m. onwards.

3. BAGGAGE.

Officers Valises to be at the Q.M. Stores ready for
loading at 8.30 a.m.

All packs and blankets rolled neatly in bundles
of ten to be at the Q.M. Stores ready for loading at 10. a.m.

4. BILLETING.

Lieut. L.A. Sale M.C. will proceed and meet D.R. O.C.
at Billet Warden's Office, LA BEUVRIERE at 10.0 a.m. 15th inst.
to arrange billeting for the Company.   Sgt. Airey 2i/c's
give him details of Coy. strength by 6. p.m. 14th inst.

5. REFILLING POINT after arrival at LA BEUVRIERE will be
ANNEZIN FOSSE 1. (F1 d. 6.6)

6. SUPPLIES. On 13th inst. there will be a second issue
at 3.0 pm for consumption on 15th inst. This will be
carried by supply wagon. On 14th inst. there will be
no issue of supplies.

Fuel available on morning of 15th inst. at
Refilling Point.

Lt. Q.M.S. will proceed with transport and arrange
to draw supplies for consumption on 15th inst.
immediately on arrival at LA BEUVRIERE.

7. BILLETS

Immediately billets in LE PREOL are evacuated on
15th inst. C.S.M. will go around with Billet Warden
and obtain from him a certificate that they have been
left in a clean and satisfactory condition. He will
hand this certificate to Adjutant immediately he has
obtained it.

8. GUM BOOTS.

All gum boots that can be spared will be cleaned
and returned to gum boot stores by 12 noon 14th inst.
Boots not handed in by that time will be retained till

3

sent is relieved and then returned to Gun Boot Store. All Gun Boots will be cleaned before being handed in to Gun Boot Store. Arrangements have been made for washing close to each Store.

J. Murray/ Capt.
O/C. 125. N. G. Coy.

Ref. Maps.
36 B. NE.
36 C. N.W.
1/20000.

125 M.G. Coy.
Reinforcement Scheme.
APPENDIX B

Secret
to be returned to orderly
room by 9 A.M. 27.2.18

No. 1.

1. General Idea.

The A.B.C. Bde has been ordered to reinforce the Camel Corps Front with all speed, and occupy defended localities behind the Village Lines. The 125 M.G. Coy is co-operating.

2. Disposition

No. 2 Sect. under Lieut J.A. Clymer & 2/Lt W.N. Strawson will co-operate with W. Bn. in the defence of the VERMELLES Locality

Only Officers, N.C.O's, No.1's and 2 runners will be included in the personnel of this Section.

No. 3 Sect. under Lt. M.A.S. Breidfjord will co-operate with Z Bn. in the defence of the ANNEQUIN Locality.

No's 1 & 4 Sects. under 2/Lt W.M. Macpherson & C.S.M. Airey. P. will co-operate with Y. Bn. in the defence of the SAILLY LA BOURSE. Locality

C. H.Q will be at Chateau des Pres. S. 27 d 65

Runners of Coy H.Q. No's 2, 3 & 4 Sects. will take bicycles

Pte. Westwell will accompany Coy. H.Q. as runner.

At 12 NOON the Enemy has broken through our front line system & is attacking the VILLAGE LINE

3. Reports.

As soon as possible after arriving in their respective Localities, each Section Officer will send a report to C.H.Q stating Situation.

Arrangements for communication with O.C. Bns
Map location of guns & cover (available or improvised).
Group H.Q. & Inf. Command Post.
Rations, water, S.A.A. supply & requirements
Disposition of Transport.

3. Reports cont.d

Sketch map shewing disposition of Inf. M.G.s & L.G.s
Hourly reports will NOT be rendered in this scheme
Each gun team will make out a range card which will be sent to O. Orderly Room on return.

4. Gun Tackle

No. 1 Section will not take gun tackle
Remainder, Both fighting limbers complete

5. Dress

Marching order less packs. Haversacks to be worn on the back. Haversack rations will be taken and water bottles full.

Note. Section Officers will take every opportunity of pointing out routes, H.Q.s etc. to their men on the march out, as well as in the Localities themselves.

The hour 12 noon to 1 p.m. will be set apart for dinners.

The scheme will cease at 3 p.m. Sections will return to billets independently.

Expected hour of return 6. p.m.

A H Carlisle Capt
p. O/c 125 M.G. Coy

No 1 O/c
" 2 2nd i/c
" 3 No 1 Sect
" 4 " 2 "
" 5 " 3 "
" 6 " 4 "
" 7 T.O
" 8 C.Q.M.S.

After Order.

Two Motor buses will be available to bring Sections back after completion of the Scheme.
They will be at

ANNEQUIN F.29 b.4.8.4. (for No's 2 & 3 Sections)
SAILLY LA BOURSE. F.27.c.89.21 (for No's 1 & 4 do)
Time 4 p.m.

Runners with bicycles will return independently
Transport will return as ordered by J.O.

(Signed) H.B. Carlisle Capt
for O.C. 135 M.G. Coy

25-2-18

To. O'C'
125 M.G. Coy.

2nd Appendix C. Copy

42 Division

> 125TH MACHINE GUN COMPANY.
> No. M.164
> Date 20/2/18

Tactical and Technical lessons learnt during the month

1. **Tactical** Nothing to report.

2. **Technical** (a) The issue of liquid prismatic compasses on the scale of 1 per section is strongly recommended in lieu of the M.K. VII prismatic compass of which two per Company are at present issued.
Reasons:— The constant need of reseecting to locate gun positions, of rapidly laying out lines of fire etc, with the greatest accuracy and speed, necessitates a steady instrument. The oil compasses fulfil these requirements.

(b) The issue of a standard folding T. shaped base of a light and portable nature for barrage drill, and also of some form of luminous aiming post is recommended.

(c) The issue of a telescopic sight for Machine Guns after the pattern of the German sight, would enable the firer to observe his own fire at medium ranges, and therefore correct errors in elevation more quickly, and would also make the gun useful for Sniping

Appendix D

Statement showing Strength of Company, Casualties etc

	OFF	OR
Strength of Co. 1st February 1918 (Including 19 OR attached)	9	148
Drafts etc	1	40
	10	218

Casualties
- Killed
- Died of Wounds
- Wounded
- Gas

	OFF	OR
Struck of strength 1 - 15	1	15
Strength of Co: Feby 28th 1918	9	203

	OFF	OR
Numbers in Field Amb: during Feby	1	21
" rejoined from "		5
" proceeded on leave	1	13
" rejoined from "	2	11
	4	50

Horses etc in possession of Co.

	OFF Chas	LD Horses	Mules
Strength 1/2/18	4	32	16
Cast	—	12	5
Drawn during month	4	20	11
		NIL	
Strength 28/2/18	4	20	11

Fire Calculations.

UNIT. 125" Machine Gun Coy. **DATE.** 6/2/18. **MAP USED.** 36c N.W. 1 (ed 10), 1/10000 LABASSÉE. **Officer i/c Firing.** Lieut. S. DICKINSON.

Gun Number & Emp. location	Target & Map location	Direction		Elevation				Clearance over own Troops					Remarks
			Grid Bearing	Contours Gun Target A.	Range to Target	V.I.	Q.E.	Range in yards corresponding to Q.E.	Distance to Own Troops	Contour Own Troops B.	Tang. Height C.	Clearance A-B+C	
A Group.													
S1. A21d 1030				Nature.			Nature.	Nearest.		Nature.			S.A.A. V49. A20d 9812.
		Close	Defence.					Furthest.					Open Emplacement. Line of Fire crosses with A 27.3; laid on Grid Bearing of 117° 30' G.
A 27.3.								Nearest.					Open Emplacement. Line of Fire crosses with S1. Laid on Grid Bearing of 53° 30' G.
A 27 c 9560		Close	Defence.					Furthest.					
A. A20d 9543	A20d 0022		125°	25	32 1900	+7	3° 37'	ROBERTSON'S ALLEY. Nearest. 475* Furthest. 925*	1925	28 30	27 45	24 40	Close Defence Position V51. A20d 9066. 113°-135°. 4 Loll Boxes 10 boxes. A. Open Emplacement.
B. A20d 9235	A28d 2805		124°	25	32 2050	+7	4° 36'	ROBERTSON'S ALLEY. Nearest. 500* Furthest. 900*	2050	28 30	34 55	31 50	Close Defence Position V52. A20d 8909. 16°-30°. 4 Loll Boxes 10 boxes. S.A.A. B. Open Emplacement.
B. Group.													
F1. A21c 7154		Close	Defence. 157°-195°.					Nearest. Furthest.					Officer i/c Firing. Lt. MTA. SALE M.C. Covered Emplacement. No 2 Brickstack.
F2. A21c 9791		Close	Defence. 157°-175°.					Nearest. Furthest.					Covered Emplacement. Altn altn. A21c 9791. 20°. 28°. No 12 Brickstack.
F3. A22a 1085		Close	Defence. 38°.					Nearest. Furthest.					Covered Emplacement. Altn altn. A22 a 1085. 177°. 182°. No 15 Brickstack. S.A.A. No 7 Brickstack. A21c 8580.

Fire Calculations

UNIT: 125 Machine Gun Coy. **DATE:** 6/2/18. **MAP USED:** 36c N.W.1 (ed. 1f) 1/10000 LA BASSÉE.

Officer i/c Firing: 2/Lt. W.N. STRAWSON.

Gun Number & Emp. Location	Target & Map Location	Direction – Grid Bearing	Elevation – Contours Gun/Target	Range to Target	V.I.	Q.E.	Range in yards corresponding to Q.E.	Distance to Own Troops	Clearance over Own Troops – Contour Int. Troops	B.	Trig. Height	C.	Clearance A-B=C	Remarks
C. Group.														
A15.1. A15.d 21.59.	Close Defence.	154°0′–184°0′	Nothing		Nothing			Nearest. Furthest.			Nothing.			S.M.G. HUIN VIEW A15.c 45.60. Traverse 30° Right.
A15.2 (day) A15.d 2261	A3.d 8060	9°–27°	25	20 2000	–5°	4°5′	1950	Nearest. OXFORD TERRACE 450. Furthest. 1100	25 28	28 50	28 47		Covered Emplacement. 3 Tilts are left at DEATH or GLORY SAP along rt & cannot use rain right. Temple down by Brig. B. Batta ad A15.2. 6 od D.T.G. Inf. A15.2. 10 " " 13? Rifle 4 " "
A15.2 (night) A16.c 0570	Close Defence.	5°						Nearest. Furthest.					A15.3	Open Emplacement. Traverse 40° Right.
F.4. A15.d 94.50	Close Defence. 151°							Nearest. Furthest.						Open Emplacement. Laid on G. Brickstack Traverse 30° Right.
A15.3.	Close Defence. 348°–9°20′							Nearest. Furthest.						Covered Emplacement. Laid on Grid Bearing of 7°30′.
A15.4.	Close Defence. 358°30′–18°							Nearest. Furthest.						Covered Emplacement. Laid on Grid Bearing of 18°.

JUNE Calculations.

Unit. 125" Trench ~ Gun Bty. DATE. 6/2/18. MAP USED. 36c N.W.1 (ed 10.) 1/10000 LA BASSÉE.
Traversing Gear E.S. Officer i/c Firing. Lt. A.L. HERRIDGE.

Gun Number & Map Location.	Target & Map Location.	Direction. Spirit Bearing.	Elevation. Contours. Gun A.	Elevation. Contours. Target.	V.I.	Q.E.	Range to Target	Range in yards corresponding to Q.E.	Clearance over Own Troops. Distance to Own Troops.	Clearance over Own Troops. Contour with Troops. B.	Clearance over Own Troops. Trig. Height. C.	Clearance over Own Troops. A-3±C.	Remarks.	Checked.
D Group.			Traversing	Traversing	Traversing			Nearest.		Traversing			S.A.A. PONT FIXE. A 14 & 2025.	
P.F.7. A14.4625	A28a 2109.	146°	21	30	2500	+9	7° 37' 2525	MARYLEBONE. Nearest. 1330"	25"	127	123	Open Emplacement. Close Defence Position. P.F.5. A14 & 5005. (covered) 350°-40°.	
								Furthest. 1975"	28	110	103		
P.F.6. A14.4622	A28c 3292.	146°	21	30	2375	+9	8° 15' 2600	MARYLEBONE. Nearest. 1300"	25	140	136	Open Emplacement. Close Defence Position. P.F.4. A14 & 6092. (covered) 1350°-1650° & 190°-1950°.	
								Furthest. 1950"	28	130	123		
V.L.56. A20c.7988	A28c 5853.	140°	22	32	2175	+10	5° 35' 2250	TOWER RESERVE. Nearest. 500"	25	64	61	Open Emplacement. Close Defence Position. Open A20c.7993 Line of Fire crossing with V.56, bearing 58°-63° G.	
								Furthest. 1450"	28	80	74		
V.L.55. A20c.7873.	A28c 7533.	140°	22	32	2225	+10	5° 48' 2275	TOWER RESERVE. Nearest. 725"	25	60	57	Open Emplacement. Close Defence Position. V.56 covered emplacement A20c.8473. Line of fire crossing with V.56.A bearing 366° G.	
								Furthest. 1350"	28	87	81		
A14.1 A14.8566.	Close Defence. 15°-55°					as Zijds 1°22'		Nearest.				Covered Emplacement. Laid on GIVENCHY CHURCH. Traverse 30° R. & L.	
								Furthest.					
A14.1 A14.7272	Traversing Fire Position.							Nearest.				Covered Emplacement arc 89°-129° G.	
								Furthest.					
S.2. A15.0445	Close Defence.					10° Zijds 30'		Nearest.				Open Emplacement. Laid 5°-0 R. of GIVENCHY CHURCH. All round Traverse.	Traversed G A15.4
								Furthest.					

www.ingramcontent.com/pod-product-compliance
Lightning Source LLC
Chambersburg PA
CBHW081356160426
43192CB00013B/2420